Air Crashes ir
193

C000152046

AIR CRASHES
IN THE
LAKE DISTRICT 1936–1976

MICHAEL J. HURST

Airlife
England

Dedication

To the airmen, airwomen and aircrew who were killed or injured in the accidents recorded in this book.

Title page: A Fairey Firefly from RNAS Anthorn, resting on the now famous Grasmere sportsfield following a forced landing.

Copyright © 1997 Michael J. Hurst

First published in the UK in 1997
by Airlife Publishing Ltd

British Library Cataloguing-in Publication Data
  A catalogue record for this book
  is available from the British Library

ISBN 1 85310 874 X

All rights reserved. No part of this book may be reproduced or transmitted in any form or by any means, electronic or mechanical including photocopying, recording or by any information storage and retrieval system, without permission from the Publisher in writing.

Typeset by Wearset, Boldon, Tyne and Wear
Printed in England by Livesey Ltd, Shrewsbury.

Airlife Publishing Ltd
101 Longden Road, Shrewsbury, SY3 9EB, England.

Contents

Preface

This book has been written with the intention of providing a chronological account of aircraft accidents which have occurred within the English Lake District; it does not imply negligence or responsibility on the part of any individual. The starting point is one of the first reported fatal accidents involving a military aircraft. The information on each incident is as accurate as possible considering the passage of time, fading memories and the reporting restrictions imposed during the Second World War. Some of the accounts are those of the aircrew involved, while others are from eyewitnesses; however, the greater portion have been taken from official military and civilian documents written at the time. After the war, reporting restrictions were lifted and many accounts can be found in local newspapers and periodicals, with the exception of some military accidents.

The author has taken a small liberty when defining the boundaries of the Lake District, so that accounts of accidents involving aircraft operating from wartime airfields within the area could be included. A number of interesting points were found during the research of material and personal accounts. Many civilians thought that any aircraft with one engine had to be a Spitfire, more than one that it must have been a Lancaster, yet the reader will find that relatively few of those types were involved. Another example was the renaming of part of the Solway Firth. The term 'Hudsons Bay' was adopted by locals because of the large number of twin-engined Hudsons which crashed in the sea. Again the reader will see that very few Hudsons actually crashed in the Solway Firth.

The author does not claim that every accident which occurred is recorded in this book. I know for certain that some aircraft have not yet been located after being reported missing in the Lakes, while wreckage has been found on fellsides and crags that has still not been positively identified. The author, a pilot himself, was also an officer in the RAFVR and visited the majority of the crash sites during the ten years of research. Other sites were visited by members of the Air Training Corps, or friends of the author. The information given with each account is as accurate as possible and includes the date, aircraft type and details, and the location of the accident; also included is the map reference when known, or an approximation. Where wreckage is known to be on site details are also given. The visitor to such locations must bear in mind that wreckage can be very difficult to find, and that much was buried by the recovery teams. The names of aircrew included in these accounts were taken from records made at the time of the investigations.

Information on some of the accidents was found to be extremely sparse, and in some cases only an official notification of a death or crash was made. Many reports did not identify the aircraft type or serial number. One such example was a forced landing at Brough. The farmer in whose field the landing was made, heard of the research into aircraft accidents and kindly sent a photograph of his family standing by the aircraft. Unfortunately the registration number was just out of camera shot and the date is uncertain; the aircraft was a Proctor Mk 3 but the incident has to be placed in the unidentified chapter.

Accident statistics

Total number of recorded accidents – 606 listed by type.

A Cadet =1	Beagle Pup = 1	F Winker Wicko = 1	McD Phantom = 1
A Tutor = 3	Beechcraft AT8 = 1	G Javelin = 1	McD Voodoo = 1
A 504k = 1	Cessna 150 = 4	G Wildcat = 2	NA Mustang = 2
A Anson = 34	Cessna 172 = 1	G Meteor = 1	NA Sabre = 1
A Auster = 4	Cherokee = 3	H Hector = 4	P Colt = 1
A Lancaster = 4	CLA-7 Swift = 1	H Henley = 1	P Proctor = 7
A Oxford = 7	D Boston = 2	H Hind = 4	PA-28 = 1
Aeronca 100 = 1	D Dakota = 5	H Hurricane = 103	PA-39 = 1
Aeronca 95 = 1	D Skyraider = 1	H Sea Fury = 1	S Stirling = 2
AW Whitley = 6	Dart Herald = 2	H Tempest = 1	SA Rallye = 1
A Horsa = 1	DH Dragonfly = 2	HP Halifax = 9	Super Aero 45 = 1
B Airacobra = 1	DH Venom = 1	HP Hampden = 9	V Valetta = 1
B Beaufighter = 46	DH Vampire = 2	HP 42 = 1	V Vildebeest = 1
B Beaufort = 13	DH Tiger Moth = 32	L Hudson = 29	V Warwick = 2
B Botha = 17	EE Canberra = 3	M Aerovan = 1	V Wellington = 40
B Expeditor = 2	EE Lightning = 1	M Geminie = 1	Vega-Gull = 1
B Sioux = 4	F Argus = 2	M Magister = 75	VS Spitfire = 25
B-17 = 2	F Barracuda = 2	M Martinet = 9	VS Walrus = 1
B-29 = 2	F Battle = 6	M Master = 9	W Lysander = 1
BA Swallow = 1	F Firefly = 2	M Messenger = 2	Unidentified = 26

■ ACCIDENTS BY YEAR

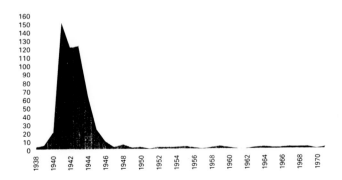

Acknowledgements

The author would like to thank all the people and various organisations that have assisted with the information, photographs and accounts that have made this book possible, in particular: MoD Directorate of Flight Safety (RAF); MoD Air Historical Branch; MoD Naval Historical Branch; MoD ARB; Public Records Office at Kew; United States Air Force; United States Navy; National Defence Headquarters of Canada; Rolls-Royce Aero-Engines Division; Cumbria Constabulary; Lancashire Constabulary; Public Archives of Canada; 1264 Squadron Air Training Corps; Mr RW Bradford; Mr SP Connatty; Mr P Connon; Mrs M Daniels; W/Cdr JCM Gibb; Mr J Huggon; and Mr GJ Rothery.

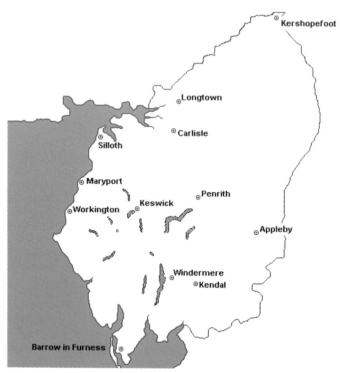

THE LAKE DISTRICT
The area of the Lake District which is covered by the book.

Chapter One

1936 to 1939

Date 21 April 1936
Aircraft DH Tiger Moth G-AARE
Location Cross Fell
Reference 684345
Aircrew Pilot AJ Moffet

Flying from RAF West Malling to Carlisle by way of Doncaster, the aircraft crashed in poor weather conditions killing its pilot. The point of impact was approximately sixty feet below the summit of Cross Fell near Appleby. The wreck remained undiscovered until the 24th when a Royal Engineers Survey team came across the wreckage. A member of the team reported that the aircraft had been smashed to matchwood; we could find no trace of the propeller so it must have disintegrated. After a number of attempts, the local police recovered the body of the pilot and burned the wreckage to prevent misreporting of the crash and to discourage souvenir hunters. A visit to the site will still reveal a few fragments of the aircraft, although it is difficult to locate in the rock field.

Date 14 June 1936
Aircraft Avro Cadet
Location St Bees Head
Reference 967113
Aircrew –

Flying from Carlisle to Croydon the pilot of this aircraft made a forced landing in a field near Blythe Place, owing to a lack of oil. The aircraft was undamaged and local villagers helped the pilot move the aircraft to high ground, and oil was obtained from a local garage. With the aircraft refilled the pilot then continued his journey.

Date 21 January 1937
Aircraft Avro 504n G-AEIJ (ex-J8705)
Location Irish Sea
Reference 001989
Aircrew Cpt N Stewart, Mechanic C Poole

En route from Belfast to Liverpool an engine failure forced the pilot to ditch his aircraft in the sea. Having seen a ship below he decided to land as close to the shore as possible; in doing so he almost hit the ship's rigging. As the pilot and his mechanic climbed out on to the wing of the aircraft a small boat from the ship arrived. As the mechanic was pulled aboard the boat the aircraft sank taking the pilot with it; attempts to save him were unsuccessful.

Date 19 April 1937
Aircraft H Hind K6617 98 Sqd 12 (F) Grp
Location Lowca
Reference 988237
Aircrew Pilot R Vaughan, Cpl WA Ballett

The crew of this aircraft had a lucky escape when they crash-landed in a field near Park House Farm, Lowca. It was one of three aircraft flying to Stranraer when they flew into heavy rain and mist. After the engine of this aircraft began to belch out black smoke while over the sea its pilot turned towards land and began a descent into a small field. As they came into land, the aircraft crashed through a hedge, tearing off its undercarriage, sliding across the ground, through another hedge before coming to a standstill.

The farmer in whose field they crashed was quickly on the scene to help the airmen, who were taken to Whitehaven hospital for treatment. The aircraft was a complete loss and the wreckage was later removed by a salvage team from its base at RAF Catterick.

Date 5 June 1937
Aircraft V Vildebeest Mk III K4607
42 Sqd
Location Shelter Crags
Reference 253055
Aircrew Sgt F Wilkinson, LAC A Mitchell

A climb to this site will still show remains of this

The crashed Vildebeest K4607 on Crinkle Craggs. The reader will see that the serial numbers on the fabric had been cut away by visitors to the site. (Mrs J Dixon)

aircraft between Crinkle Ghyll and Three Tarns on Shelter Crags, where it crashed killing its crew while flying from Filton to Donibristle. They encountered poor weather conditions during the flight and it took rescue teams a number of days to locate the aircraft and recover the bodies of the crew.

Date   5 June 1937
Aircraft   H Hind K6614 98 Sqd
Location   Threshthwaite Cove
Reference   428108
Aircrew   Sgt S Mitchell, LAC G Murray
The same poor weather conditions that were responsible for the previous crash also sealed the fate of this aircraft and its crew. Villagers living in Hartsop described hearing an aircraft fly low over the village and into the valley during the night but did not hear it climb out. The aircraft had flown into the fellside at Threshthwaite Cove above Hartsop village, and remains of this aircraft can still be found at the crash site.

A squadron of eleven aircraft had left RAF West Freugh for various stations around the country; three of the eleven crashed en route, one of which was K6614. One crashed at Port William, the second at Haines Hill, Berkshire, while another made a forced landing in the River Dee, Kirkcudbrightshire.

Date   8 July 1937
Aircraft   Aeronca G-AEXB
Location   Irish Sea
Reference   931262
Aircrew   R Grubb
This aircraft and its pilot were reported missing over the Irish Sea, the last position given as 'off Whitehaven'. Neither has been seen since. The pilot of this aircraft won the 1936 Folkstone Trophy race at a speed of 84.75 mph.

Date   11 September 1937
Aircraft   Comper CLA-7 Swift G-AAZD
Location   Ravenglass
Reference   053970
Aircrew   Sqd Ldr Atcherly
While competing in the King's Cup air race, an

The wreckage of the Hawker Hind on Threshthwaite Cove. Sections of the aircraft's fabric with its Squadron markings have been cut away by souvenir hunters. (Mr TA Fawcett)

engine failure forced the pilot to make an emergency landing on the beach at Ravenglass. Local people assisted the pilot in pulling the aircraft up the beach and out of the reach of the incoming tide. A mechanic from the Border Flying Club later repaired the engine and the aircraft left a short time later for Blackpool.

Date 26 November 1937
Aircraft H Hind K6632 218 Sqd
Location Workington
Reference 983285
Aircrew P/O EA Hunt, AC A Merioneth
Flying from Edinburgh to Hooton, this aircraft developed an engine failure while over the Irish Sea. The pilot turned towards land at a height of around 100 feet. He flew parallel with the shore to avoid hitting the slag bank at Workington, and was forced to ditch the aircraft in eight feet of water. The aircraft somersaulted on hitting the

water, but both crew managed to free themselves from the plane. The pilot was seen trying to swim ashore with his observer on his back. Sadly, both men went underwater and drowned only a short distance from land. The aircraft, based at RAF Upper Heyford, was later salvaged.

Date 14 May 1938
Aircraft P-10 Vega Gull G-AFGU
Location Keswick
Reference 284249
Aircrew Pilot S Smith, R Radcliffe, N Ayton
There are a number of accounts of this accident, but it appears that the aircraft emerged from low cloud and made a steep turn to avoid hitting a fell top after which parts began to fall from the tail unit. The aircraft then crashed into the lower slopes of Latrigg bursting into flames, killing its

crew of three from the Newcastle Flying Club.

A fell walker both heard and then found the crashed plane; its engine was buried several feet into the ground and the majority of the wreckage was removed a few days later.

Date 16 May 1938
Aircraft Unidentified
Location Bootle
Reference 100902
Aircrew Pilot Sgt Blacklock + ANO

Shortly before it was to take up duties at the weapons testing range, this aircraft had to make an emergency landing in a field near Seaton Hall. The aircraft struck a hedge while landing and spun into the ground. Its undercarriage, wings and propeller were badly damaged, though the pilot and his observer escaped unhurt.

A recovery vehicle and crew was sent to dismantle and recover the aircraft, but it broke down at the scene. Spare parts for the repair of the truck were parachuted from another aircraft on the 20th.

Date 20 June 1938
Aircraft BA Swallow
Location Workington
Reference 007297
Aircrew –

A well known lady flier of her day, en route from Blackpool to Carlisle, made a forced landing in a field near Workington after encountering poor weather conditions. Following an overnight stay and an improvement in the weather, she continued her journey the next day.

Date 3 January 1939
Aircraft G Gladiator K7998 25 Sqd 11 Grp
Location Great Corby
Reference 484537
Aircrew P/O G Evans

A fuel shortage caused the pilot of this aircraft to make a forced landing in a field near Keepers Cottage; when almost down the aircraft struck a tree, ripping off a wing and crashing into the ground.

The aircraft was completely wrecked yet the

Unidentified P Proctor photographed by the owner of Field Head Farm, in whose field it made a forced landing.

pilot escaped with only facial cuts and bruises. The remains of the aircraft were recovered by a salvage team. At the time of the accident the aircraft was flying from RAF Unsworth.

Date 20 January 1939
Aircraft F Battle
Location Seascale
Reference 036034
Aircrew Pilot P/O Jacobie

A mechanical failure caused the aircraft to make a forced landing in a field near Calder Hall. A maintenance crew later repaired the aircraft on site and it was flown out to Stranraer on the 24th.

Date 19 July 1939
Aircraft VS Spitfire Mk I K9888 41 Sqd
Location Dunn Fell
Reference 705319
Aircrew Sgt K Mitchell

While on a training flight from RAF Catterick to Dumfries, this aircraft crashed into a fell side above the Silver Band Mines.

Workers at the mine recounted how they heard an aircraft roar overhead, followed by a loud explosion. As they hurried to the crash site they came across metal fragments strewn over a wide area and found a large crater. The body of the pilot was found some distance from the impact site, and though most of the wreckage was taken away, a few fragments can still be located.

Date 29 July 1939
Aircraft DH 86A L7596 (ex-G-ADYJ)
Location Kirby in Furness
Reference 246815
Aircrew (Sir Kingsley Wood)

The Secretary of State for Air was one of the passengers on this ex-British Airways aircraft flying to Belfast. Radio contact was lost after a report by its radio operator which advised that the pilot was going to attempt a forced landing due to poor weather, at Out Park. An air/sea search was started in the Barrow and Morecambe bay areas, and the aircraft was located on level ground near Harlock Farm above Kirby in Furness. The VIP escaped the crash with only a few cuts and shock and he spent time at Kirby vicarage until transport arrived.

A guard was posted on the wreckage until it was later removed by a salvage team from RAF Sealand.

Chapter Two
The war years

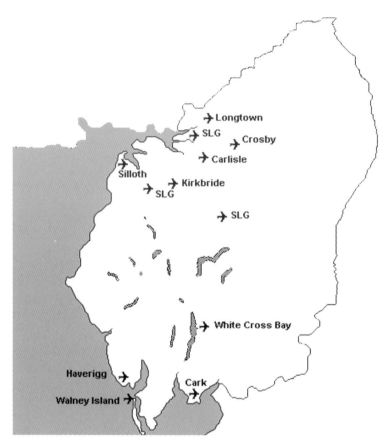

Operational airfields within the author's Lake District

Date 29 November 1939
Aircraft V Wellington L4388 22 MU
V Wellington L4389 22 MU
Location Silloth
Reference 128543
Aircrew –
The pilot of L4388 was making an emergency landing at RAF Silloth following an engine failure when he crashed into the second aircraft which was waiting on the runway. Both aircraft were badly damaged but the crews were unhurt.

Date 15 January 1940
Aircraft A Tutor K4820 16 Grp
A Tutor Unidentified
Location Alston
Reference 653425
Aircrew –
Two aircraft on a training flight got into difficulties near Alston. The pilot of one aircraft managed to make a forced landing on the fell top at Hartside quite close to the main road.
The second pilot was not so lucky and had to bale out; he landed safely although his aircraft crashed and burned out near Slaggie Ford.

Date 23 February 1940
Aircraft A Tutor K4800
Location Bowness on Windermere
Reference 419955
Aircrew F/Lt GAB Cooper AC Bassow
Flying from RAF Kenly to RAF Kirkbride the oil pressure dropped to zero, the pilot made a forced landing in a field near the 'Oaks'. Damage to the aircraft was a broken propeller, twisted undercarriage and bent wings.
The crew of two were shaken but unhurt, and a police guard was placed on the aircraft until a salvage team from RAF Silloth removed it.

Date 2 March 1940
Aircraft DH 87 Hornet Moth X9325
(G-ADNA)
Location Penrith
Reference 584404
Aircrew –
After being impressed into military service and while still being delivered, the aircraft made a forced landing in a field near Glassonby. The

crew were unhurt and continued their journey by road. The aircraft was later recovered by a salvage unit and remained in service with the RAF until 1946, when it was returned to civil aviation.

Date 6 March 1940
Aircraft H Hind K6655 142 Sqd
Location Cockermouth
Reference 206344
Aircrew P/O Armstrong
While attempting an emergency landing in rough pasture, the aircraft overturned and came to rest against a hedge near Irton House. Its crew escaped with only minor injuries.

Date 3 June 1940
Aircraft F Battle P2157 15 EFTS
Location Kingstown
Reference 392594
Aircrew AC Okie
Following several attempts to land, the pilot eventually managed to crash the aircraft onto the airfield. After making his 'landing' the pilot was arrested as he proved to be unqualified, and had taken the aircraft for a short trip.

Date 17 July 1940
Aircraft M Magister 15 EFTS
Location River Esk
Reference 345646
Aircrew –
The pilot of this aircraft was killed after flying into power cables and pylons, then crashing into the river. Witnesses who saw the accident reported that the pilot had been seen to fly beneath the cables twice before his third and fatal attempt. The wreckage was removed by a local salvage unit.

Date 22 July 1940
Aircraft M Magister Mk I T9738 15 EFTS
Location Mossband
Reference 351657
Aircrew –
During a training flight this aircraft crash-landed north of Carlisle at Mossband. The pilot was unhurt and the aircraft recovered by road transport a short time later.

Date 22 July 1940
Aircraft M Magister Mk I P6412 15 EFTS
Location Kingstown
Reference 392594
Aircrew –
Same day, same type of aircraft, but this time a crash-landing on Kingstown airfield. Crash units recovered both aircraft and pilot.

Date 25 July 1940
Aircraft B Beaufighter W1088
Location Unknown
Reference –
Aircrew Pilot RAD Smith
The pilot of this aircraft was killed in a crash-landing. He was ferrying the aircraft from RAF Kirkbride to Dumfries when the starboard engine caught fire.

Date 25 July 1940
Aircraft BL Botha Mk I L6124
Location Cockermouth
Reference 168367
Aircrew P/O Bradshaw
After mechanical problems the pilot decided to make a forced landing on rough pasture at Therepland Moss; the aircraft was badly damaged but its crew escaped without serious injury. The aircraft was removed by a salvage unit.

Date 26 July 1940
Aircraft M Magister Mk I L8336
Location Kingstown
Reference 392594
Aircrew –
A heavy landing following a training flight caused severe structural damage to the under-carriage of this aircraft. The pilot was unhurt and the aircraft repaired on site.

Date 7 August 1940
Aircraft HP 42 G-AAUC (HORSA)
AS981 271 Sqd
Location Moresby Parks
Reference 006210
Aircrew Pilot P/O EG Libbey
This is the pilot's own account of this incident

involving an ex-Imperial Airways aircraft impressed into military service:

I took off from Doncaster airport in an HP 47 AS981 from 271 Squadron heading for Ringway airport. I was scheduled to pick up a cargo of three thousand pounds of ammunition (in boxes) including tracer etc., which was destined for a base in the Hebrides. My crew consisted of a second pilot and two airmen, a fitter and a rigger who were in the rear part of the aircraft passenger accommodation. From Ringway we set course for Prestwick via St Bees Head and all went well to that point.

As we were heading out to sea, the top starboard engine cut out suddenly; my second pilot rushed to the rear of the cockpit to juggle with the petrol cocks as I altered course to fly along the coast. It was about then that my second pilot stuck his head out of the cockpit window and saw the starboard upper engine on fire. A few moments later the starboard lower engine cut out and we were really in trouble. At a height of 1,500 feet above high cliffs, we were faced with two choices: either to throttle back and land into wind amid large rocks, or to keep full power on the starboard engines and stagger on at a horribly low airspeed until we were heading almost downwind towards some rough-looking high ground a short distance inland, where I hoped to make a reasonable forced landing before we fell out of the sky.

I decided on the latter just as the starboard upper and lower wings started burning. I have a memory of flying very low over a bus going along a narrow road, probably scaring everybody to death. I made quite a nice landing in a rough field. Unfortunately after running a short distance we ran into what I think might have been an old Roman earthwork, something like a brick and grass covered wall several feet high running at right angles across our field. This smashed our undercarriage and we slid to a standstill on the fuselage alone; luckily neither of us was injured but a hurried evacuation of the aircraft was obvious since it was now well alight. We could not escape back down the fuse-lage since the ammunition boxes were piled up against the back of the door leading from the forward cabin into the cockpit. We had to squeeze through the small windows in the cockpit, heaven knows how we did it, then we dashed towards the main fuselage door to find out what had happened to the two crewmen. Before we got there, however, we were surprised and pleased to find them rushing towards us on a similar mission.

I noticed that the aircraft had come to rest in a saucer-like basin in the ground, which would help to give some protection when the ammunition started to go off. I told everyone to get well out of the way and lie on some dead ground. We then saw an army officer and his platoon rushing towards the aircraft, presumably looking for us. We managed to attract their attention and show them that we were all right just before the fireworks started to go off and the aircraft became a mass of flames. The army personnel subsequently came in very useful in providing a guard right around the crash site. I duly phoned the maintenance unit at RAF Carlisle, which was the nearest RAF unit, and they sent down the necessary guard and relief personnel. After a short time the wreckage was later removed by a salvage unit.

Date	24 August 1940
Aircraft	BL Botha Mk 1 L6160 1c OTU
Location	Silloth
Reference	119515
Aircrew	P/O D Alexander 9093
	Sgt D Lowry 94493
	Sgt K Thompson 742868 ANO

The crew of this aircraft perished when it crashed and burned out while taking part in a night flying exercise. The crash site was near Balladoyle Farm, which subsequently became noted for aircraft crashes.

Date	28 August 1940
Aircraft	BL Botha Mk II L6203 1c OTU
Location	Silloth
Reference	119515
Aircrew	–

Aircraft crashed at Balladoyle Farm killing its crew of three. No further information is available on this accident.

Date	22 September 1940
Aircraft	M Magister Mk I L8076
	15 EFTS
	M Magister Mk I T9713
	15 EFTS
Location	Kingstown
Reference	932594
Aircrew	–

Both of these aircraft were written off in a flying accident on the airfield; no other details were recorded.

Date	29 September 1940
Aircraft	S Stirling
Location	Barbon
Reference	622827
Aircrew	–

Following a hazardous low-level flight down the valleys of the Pennines, brought about by a combination of low fuel and loss of direction, the pilot managed to make a successful crash-landing in a field near to the main road at Barbon. Of the crew of six, four were seriously injured and after treatment by a local doctor they were taken to Lancaster hospital by ambulance. The aircraft remained under guard for some time until removed by a salvage unit.

Date	5 October 1940
Aircraft	W Lysander Mk II N1295
Location	Kirby Stephen
Reference	785091
Aircrew	P/O H Thomas

Flying from Inverness, the pilot encountered poor weather conditions and made an emergency landing in a field near Hartly Fold. As the aircraft touched down, it crashed into a low stone wall. Its crew climbed out unhurt and the aircraft was later removed by a salvage team.

Date	17 October 1940
Aircraft	V Wellington Mk Ic L7857
	75NZ Sqd 3 Grp
Location	Penrith
Reference	521371
Aircrew	–

The crew abandoned this aircraft after getting into difficulties nearing Penrith. All landed safely by parachute at various sites around the town. The aircraft, however, continued on until it hit flat ground on Brown Rigg near Plumpton. A visit to this site will still show a large discoloured patch of soil resulting from the intense fire which followed the impact. The aircraft was carrying a load of bombs and mines which burned fiercely. A machine-gun from the aircraft was found in 1973 sticking out from the soft ground near the impact point.

Date 26 October 1940
Aircraft M Magister Mk I R1850 15 EFTS
M Magister Mk I R1846 15 EFTS
M Magister Mk I R1853 15 EFTS
M Magister Mk I R1904 15 EFTS
M Magister Mk I T9736 15 EFTS
Location Carlisle
Reference 392594
Aircrew NF Knight 1301942
L Harrod 1301895 + ANO
R Holled 1302067
C Nepean-Bishop

All of these aircraft crashed not only on the same day but within a few minutes of each other. The accidents occurred as the flight was taking off in formation from Kingstown airfield. One hit a pile of stones by the boundary fence, which removed the undercarriage, the aircraft stopping in the middle of the Glasgow Road. The second just got airborne but hit two fences and crashed in the field beyond. Number three stopped short of the fence having lost its undercarriage and then ran into a small tent. The fourth climbed to about ten feet, stalled and hit a small hangar. The fifth staggered across the road and hit the roof of a bungalow depositing its engine on the occupant's bed. The aircrews were unhurt but three ground crew were killed as one aircraft ran through their tent. The cause of the accidents was attributed to hoarfrost on the wings of the aircraft.

Date 26 November 1940
Aircraft A Anson Mk I W1790
Location Kingstown
Reference 388359
Aircrew –

Following a second attempt to land this aircraft, and being unable to maintain flying speed, the pilot made a crash-landing south-west of the airfield near a small wood. The crew were unhurt but before the aircraft could be removed local children set fire to it and it burned out on 1 December.

Date 31 December 1940
Aircraft M Magister Mk I L8355
15 EFTS
Location Ullswater
Reference 435206
Aircrew –

While carrying out unauthorised aerobatics and low flying over the lake, the wheels of this aircraft touched the surface of the water, causing it to spin into the lake. The pilot managed to escape from the cockpit and swam ashore in his flying suit, which was quite a considerable task in the cold water. Meanwhile, the aircraft sank to the bottom of the lake never to be seen again until a combined team of Air Cadets and divers recovered it in 1974. Due to the amount of time it had spent under water, it quickly began to disintegrate on contact with fresh air. The wreckage was taken to the Air Cadet Headquarters in Windermere and reconstructed. The photograph shows the recovery of the wreckage and the 'reconstructed' aircraft

Date 7 January 1941
Aircraft B Botha Mk I L6126
Location Irish Sea
Reference 930178
Aircrew –

During a training flight from its base at RAF Silloth, this aircraft ditched in the sea off Whitehaven. Although a large-scale search was carried out, its crew were never found.

Date 16 January 1941
Aircraft M Magister Mk I R1843
15 EFTS
Location Solway Firth
Reference 172619
Aircrew DM Crook

An engine failure during a training flight caused this pilot to make a forced landing on the sands of the Solway. He was unhurt although the aircraft was lost.

The instrument panel of the Magister is recovered from Ullswater by ATC cadets and divers. Unfortunately the aircraft, being mainly wooden, began to disintegrate during the lift from the lake bed.
(MJ Hurst)

Date	21 January 1941
Aircraft	M Magister Mk I T9687
	15 EFTS
Location	Kingstown
Reference	392594
Aircrew	–

The pilot escaped unhurt after the aircraft overturned while he was attempting to take-off out of wind. Airfield crash teams recovered the aircraft later the same day.

Date	1 February 1941
Aircraft	H Hurricane Mk I P3658 258 Sqd
	9 Grp
Location	Newby
Reference	578220
Aircrew	–

Shortly after flying into a blizzard the aircraft's engine began to fail; the pilot made a forced landing in a field near Syke House Farm at Newby. The aircraft was one of five flying to

RAF Jurby in the Isle of Man. The pilot was unhurt and the aircraft removed a short time later.

Date	4 February 1941
Aircraft	DH Tiger Moth Mk II T7055
	15 EFTS
Location	Kingstown
Reference	392594
Aircrew	Pilot Ritchards

Landing on a snow-covered airfield the aircraft skidded and overturned; the pilot was unhurt and the plane recovered by a crash team.

Date	12 February 1941
Aircraft	V Wellington
Location	Greyrigg
Reference	584037
Aircrew	–

Shortly after three in the morning this aircraft began to run low on fuel, its crew baled out near

The author and cadets part way through the reconstruction of the Ullswater Magister. (MJ Hurst)

Tebay. They were collected and taken to hospital at Grange-over-Sands for checks. The aircraft continued on alone until it crashed into the fell side above Betherdale Hall and exploded. The majority of the wreckage was removed by salvage teams although a few fragments can still be located.

Date	26 February 1941
Aircraft	F Battle
Location	Methop
Reference	456812
Aircrew	–

A mechanical failure in the aircraft caused the pilot to make a forced landing near the sanatorium at Methop. Although the aircraft was badly damaged the pilot was unhurt and the aircraft was recovered by a salvage team.

Date	8 March 1941
Aircraft	BL Botha Mk I L6262
Location	Millom
Reference	140790
Aircrew	–

Aircraft crashed and burned out. No further information available.

Date	18 March 1941
Aircraft	M Magister Mk I N3836 15 EFTS
Location	Kingstown
Reference	392594
Aircrew	–

Shortly after take-off this aircraft suffered an engine failure. The pilot tried to return to the airfield but crashed short of the runway. He was not badly injured but the aircraft was a complete loss.

The war years

Date   21 March 1941
Aircraft   H Hurricane
Location   Hawkshead
Reference 364995
Aircrew   –
A young American pilot on a training flight made a forced landing on the lower slopes of Latterbarrow due to a fuel shortage. Neither pilot nor machine was damaged and the aircraft was later removed by road.

Date   25 March 1941
Aircraft   V Wellington Mk Ic T2712
               21 OTU
Location   Frizington
Reference 041184
Aircrew   –
During a delivery flight from RAF Moreton-in-the-Marsh the aircraft developed engine trouble and made a crash-landing at night near Heather Lea at Frizington. It hit telephone lines and crashed on the main road. Its crew escaped uninjured and the aircraft was fairly well intact. It was removed by road by a salvage unit from RAF Silloth.

Date   27 March 1941
Aircraft   M Master Mk I T8822 1 FPS
Location   St Bees Head
Reference 951129
Aircrew   1st Off GW Holcomb
An American ATA pilot died after his aircraft crashed into Tomlin Point near St Bees and burned out. The wreckage was removed by a salvage unit.

Date   27 March 1941
Aircraft   M Magister Mk I R1966 15 EFTS
Location   Solway Firth
Reference 196618
Aircrew   –
After losing control of his aircraft in cloud, the pilot made a forced landing on the foreshore at Silloth. Its crew were unhurt and the aircraft was returned to its base later, by a salvage team.

Date   31 March 1941
Aircraft   H Hurricane Mk I V7537
               H Hurricane Mk I V6987
Location   Scarr Craggs
               Birkdale Fell
Reference 212208 366170
Aircrew   F/O JW Seddon, P/O TC Smith
               61251
Two pilots were flying from RAF Northolt to RAF Crosby delivering these aircraft and collecting two new Mk IIs, with which their Squadron was re-equipping. Their flight path brought them up the coast and across the Lake District near Keswick, where they flew into a blizzard. One of the aircraft flew into Scarr Craggs exploding on impact. The second flew on towards Ullswater where it too crashed and burned out on Birkdale Fell. Of the two sites only Scarr Craggs shows remains of the aircraft which are scattered down a scree slope, from the still quite visible impact point. The remains are small and care should be taken as ammunition is still lying around in the rocks.

Date   31 March 1941
Aircraft   M Magister Mk I N3856
               15 EFTS
Location   Monkhill
Reference 339583
Aircrew   –
An engine failure during aerobatic manoeuvres caused the pilot to make a forced landing on marshland at Monkhill. The pilot was unhurt and the aircraft later removed by a salvage team.

Date   12 April 1941
Aircraft   A Oxford Mk II T1201
Location   Keswick
Reference 234228
Aircrew   F/O CWR Sawer 41212,
               F/Lt RE Brice 43334, Sgt FJ Bliss
               (wop) 91225, B Larson
After taking off from RAF Kingstown, the crew of this aircraft lost their lives when the aircraft crashed into Little Braithwaite Wood near Keswick, known locally as Johnny Wood. Apart from the poor weather in the area at the time of the accident little else is known about the cause

of the crash. It now takes an exacting search to find any trace of the wreckage.

Date   12 April 1941
Aircraft   H Hurricane Mk I P3831
                 59 OTU
Location   Longtown
Reference   340228
Aircrew   F/O BW Vickers 42282

The pilot of this aircraft thought he had a major airframe failure when he heard a loud and continuous banging sound. He baled out of his aircraft, but hit the tailplane and was instantly killed. The aircraft crashed and burned out at Mill Hill near Longtown. An investigation later proved the banging noise to have been caused by a lose inspection panel.

Date   14 April 1941
Aircraft   M Magister
Location   Lowther Park
Reference   521232
Aircrew   –

A fuel shortage was the cause of this forced landing in Lowther Park. The aircraft was later refuelled and returned to its base the same day.

Date   14 April 1941
Aircraft   M Magister Mk I R1967 15 EFTS
Location   Kingstown
Reference   408588
Aircrew   –

Mechanical failure caused the pilot to make an emergency landing at Hadrians Camp near Carlisle. The crew were unhurt, but a husband and wife out walking in the area, Mr and Mrs FJ Boul, were killed as the aircraft landed.

Date   14 April 1941
Aircraft   BL Botha Mk 1 L6283
Location   Millom
Reference   140790
Aircrew   –

A report in the station log is the only record showing that this aircraft crashed shortly after take-off.

Date   15 April 1941
Aircraft   BL Botha Mk I L6431
                 F Battle Mk I L5785
Location   Millom
Reference   140790
Aircrew   –

Following a mid-air collision both aircraft managed to make crash-landings at RAF Haverigg. Airfield crash teams recovered the wreckage.

Date   18 April 1941
Aircraft   M Magister Mk 1 L8328
Location   Southwaite
Reference   432457
Aircrew   –

Aerobatics at a low height and an engine failure resulted in the aircraft crashing a mile from the railway station at Southwaite. The wreckage was removed by a salvage team

Date   25 April 1941
Aircraft   H Hurricane 59 OTU
Location   Kingstown
Reference   392594
Aircrew   –

An engine failure during a training flight caused the pilot to make a crash-landing on Kingstown airfield; the pilot was unhurt and the aircraft was returned into service following repair.

Date   26 April 1941
Aircraft   L Hudson Mk I P5147
Location   Unknown
Reference   Unknown
Aircrew   F/O WD Whatley 44199

Although there is a record of this aircraft crashing in the Lake District, no other firm information can be traced.

Date   2 May 1941
Aircraft   M Magister Mk I P2470 15 EFTS
                 M Magister Mk I T9687 15 EFTS
Location   Kingstown
Reference   392594
Aircrew   –

These aircraft crashed into each other during take-off. The crews were unhurt though the aircraft were badly damaged.

Date 4 May 1941
Aircraft L Hudson Mk I N7304
Location Solway Firth
Reference 145596
Aircrew P/O MS Smith 89356
This aircraft crashed into the Solway Firth and sank killing its crew. No other information is available.

Date 6 May 1941
Aircraft H Hurricane Mk I V6921
312 Sqd
Location Fraggs Craggs, Burnbank
Reference 118219
Aircrew Sgt BV Volruba 787435
After getting into difficulties on a flight to the Isle of Man, the pilot was advised to bale out of his aircraft. He did not do so and was killed when it crashed into Burnbank near Loweswater. The majority of the wreckage was removed by a salvage team.

Date 18 May 1941
Aircraft M Magister Mk I R1852
15 EFTS
Location Burnfoot
Reference 370660
Aircrew J Szabunienica
The student pilot of this aircraft was killed during a training flight when he crashed on Burnfoot airfield.

Date 20 May 1941
Aircraft H Hurricane Mk I V7043
Location Kingstown
Reference 392594
Aircrew –
Seconds after take-off this aircraft was badly damaged when the pilot crashed onto the airfield.

Date 4 June 1941
Aircraft H Hurricane Mk I V6632
59 OTU
Location Carlisle
Reference 342619
Aircrew DE Fletcher
Salvage units removed the wreckage of this aircraft after it crashed at Rockcliff, north of Carlisle, while on a training flight. Its student pilot was killed.

Date 5 June 1941
Aircraft M Magister Mk 14a R1845
15 EFTS
Location Kingstown
Reference 392594
Aircrew –
An engine failure during its approach to land caused the aircraft to crash onto the airfield. The pilot was unhurt but the aircraft was badly damaged.

Date 7 June 1941
Aircraft H Hurricane Mk I W9131
59 OTU
Location Kingstown
Reference 392594
Aircrew –
Too high an airspeed while landing caused the aircraft to crash on the field; the pilot was unhurt, the aircraft suffered minor damage. It was repaired on site and returned into service a few days later. However, as the reader will note, it crashed again on the eighteenth.

Date 8 June 1941
Aircraft H Hurricane Mk I R4098
59 OTU
H Hurricane Mk I P3034
59 OTU
Location Kingstown
Reference 392594
Aircrew –
Both pilots made bad landings while on training flights; one hit and went through the boundary fence and the other managed to stop just short. R4098 was destroyed in an accident at Cumortrae killing its pilot in May 1942. P3034 had a further accident in October 1942.

Date 18 June 1941
Aircraft H Hurricane Mk I W9131 59 OTU
Location Craggs
Reference 305462
Aircrew Sgt AP Kitherside
On a training flight from RAF Annan, this pilot was killed when the aircraft crashed eight miles west of Carlisle at Craggs. The wreckage was removed by a salvage unit. The reader will see this aircraft was involved in the previous accident.

Date 20 June 1941
Aircraft VS Spitfire Mk I N3265
Location Kingstown
Reference 392594
Aircrew –
This aircraft overshot the runway while landing and ran through the perimeter fence. Salvage teams removed the aircraft.

Date 22 June 1941
Aircraft BP Defiant Mk I AA306 6 FPP
Location Gilsland
Reference 625677
Aircrew –
Flown by an ATA pilot en route to its base, the aircraft crashed near Gilsland. Locals reported seeing the aircraft flying very low just before the crash occurred. The wreckage was taken away by a salvage unit.

Date 25 June 1941
Aircraft H Hurricane Mk I V7044 59 OTU
Location Kershopefoot
Reference 475825
Aircrew JB Spangler R71573
This aircraft was destroyed and its pilot killed when it crashed at Kershopefoot near Newcastleton. The wreckage was removed by a salvage unit.

Date 25 June 1941
Aircraft M Magister Mk I L8084
15 EFTS
Location Carlisle
Reference 396591
Aircrew A Habola
Following a structural failure during aerobatics, the pilot of this aircraft baled out near Park Broom. Almost at once the aircraft broke up and crashed onto the village. The pilot escaped from the aircraft and landed safely by parachute.

Date 25 June 1941
Aircraft AW Whitley Mk III K8974
Location Kingstown
Reference 392594
Aircrew –
Following a landing on the airfield the pilot taxied into a parked Magister aircraft. Both aircraft were damaged but repaired later on site.

Date 26 June 1941
Aircraft H Hurricane Mk I V6669 59 OTU
Location Ivegill
Reference 432468
Aircrew –
Wreckage from this aircraft is still on site in soft ground near Thackwood. It crashed during a routine training flight from RAF Crosby. Complete recovery was not possible due to the soft ground in the area.

Date 1 July 1941
Aircraft M Magister Mk I N5432 15 EFTS
Location Carlisle
Reference 392594
Aircrew –
After landing on the airfield the pilot taxied into another aircraft damaging the starboard wing.

Date 1 July 1941
Aircraft DH Tiger Moth Mk II T7730
15 EFTS
Location Beaumont
Reference 344597
Aircrew –
An engine failure during aerobatics led to a forced landing in a field at Beaumont. The pilot was unhurt and the aircraft was recovered later.

Date 4 July 1941
Aircraft H Hurricane Mk I V6996
59 OTU
Location Carlisle
Reference 385675
Aircrew Sgt FG Nanke 1375405
The pilot was killed and wreckage scattered over a wide area after it crashed near Howend, Carlisle. Crash and salvage teams removed the wreckage over a period of days.

Date 8 July 1941
Aircraft M Magister Mk I V1081
15 EFTS
Location Thursby
Reference 338466
Aircrew Cpl M Peszynskie
A Polish pilot under training was supposed to have been carrying out an air test in this aircraft when he crashed into a small wood

at Green Quarries, Thursby. At the time of the accident he was carrying out unauthorised aerobatics and entered a spin from which he was unable to recover. The wreckage was later removed.

Date 14 July 1941
Aircraft AW Whitley Mk I X6748
Location Anthorn
Reference –
Aircrew –
During an air test flight from RAF Kirkbride, this aircraft made a forced landing near Solway House because of poor weather. The crew were unhurt but the aircraft was badly damaged, it was later removed by road.

Date 16 July 1941
Aircraft AW Whitley Mk V P4971
Location Silloth
Reference 126542
Aircrew Pilot Sgt C Odonell, Sgt AH Green (wop) 950638,
Pilot Sgt AE Wittbourne 400164
Rescue teams were quickly on the scene after this aircraft crashed at RAF Silloth, they managed to release two of the crew but the third, the wireless operator, had been killed in the impact. Sadly the two crew who were rescued later died in hospital.

Date 16 July 1941
Aircraft F Battle Mk I L5775 10 BGS
Location Solway Firth
Reference 103640
Aircrew LAC W Weatherburn 640401
While carrying out gunnery practice the aircraft crashed onto Blackshaw Bank killing one of its crew.

Date 17 July 1941
Aircraft M Magister Mk I R1844
15 EFTS
Location Kingstown
Reference 392594
Aircrew –
This aircraft stalled at a height of twenty feet crashing down onto the airfield. Although the aircraft was badly damaged the pilot was unhurt.

Date 18 July 1941
Aircraft H Hurricane Mk I V7534
59 OTU
Location Appleby
Reference 391593
Aircrew P/O JK Roberts RCAF
Wreckage from this aircraft can still be seen near the shooting box, close to great Rundale Tarn. Its Canadian pilot was killed and wreckage was scattered over a wide area.

Date 22 July 1941
Aircraft M Magister Mk I R1968
15 EFTS
Location Kingstown
Reference 391593
Aircrew –
This aircraft is recorded as crashing one hundred yards north of the airfield; no other information was given. It was repaired on site.

Date 23 July 1941
Aircraft H Hurricane Mk I V7674
15 EFTS
Location Kingstown
Reference 392594
Aircrew –
Landing too quickly down hill and out of wind the aircraft overturned on the airfield. The pilot was shaken but unhurt.

Date 24 July 1941
Aircraft M Magister Mk I R1905 15 EFTS
Location Burnfoot
Reference 371665
Aircrew –
A report exists in the day diary that this aircraft crashed on Burnfoot airfield. No other details were recorded.

Date 24 July 1941
Aircraft H Hurricane Mk I
15 EFTS
Location Burnfoot
Reference 371665
Aircrew –
The pilot escaped unhurt after he crashed his aircraft on Burnfoot airfield during a training sortie. The plane was extensively damaged.

Date 25 July 1941
Aircraft M Magister Mk I P6398 15 EFTS
M Magister Mk I T1968
15 EFTS
Location Kingstown
Reference 392594
Aircrew –
Two accidents occurred on this day. The first aircraft made a heavy landing, damaging its undercarriage which then collapsed; the starboard wing was also ripped off. The second occurred when a student pilot overshot the runway when landing, crashing through the perimeter fence. Its crew were unhurt.

Date 28 July 1941
Aircraft L Hudson Mk II T9268
Location Skinburness
Reference 149569
Aircrew F/O CT Dacombe 43199,
Sgt L Larsen 932979
The bodies of two airmen were recovered from the sands near Grune Point after the aircraft they were flying crashed during a training flight.

Date 29 July 1941
Aircraft H Hurricane Mk I V7255
59 OTU
Location Esk Bridge
Reference 351645
Aircrew Sgt HS Jacques 968333
A Sergeant flying instructor was killed when this aircraft crashed near the Esk Bridge, north of Carlisle. Salvage teams removed the wreckage a few days later.

Date 29 July 1941
Aircraft H Hurricane Mk I L1870
59 OTU
Location Aspatria
Reference 192430
Aircrew –
This aircraft crash-landed in a field near Watch Hill. It was later recovered by a salvage team.

Date 1 August 1941
Aircraft A Anson Mk I N5093
Location Appleby
Reference 648275
Aircrew –

The crew of five escaped without injury when the aircraft made a forced landing on Whiteacre Top near Low Appleby. The aircraft was on transport duties with the ATA at the time of the accident.

Date 3 August 1941
Aircraft BP Defiant Mk 1 N1736 2 FPP
Location Penrith
Reference 548288
Aircrew P/O Cragg
Flying from RAF St Athen to Prestwick, the pilot made a crash-landing in a field near the Beacon café on the A66, due to engine failure. The pilot was unhurt and the aircraft removed by road.

Date 12 August 1941
Aircraft H Hurricane Mk I V7742
H Hurricane Mk I V6565
Location Scafell
Reference 209049 211049
Aircrew Sgt S Karubin 793420,
P/O Z Hohne P0875
Wreckage can still be found from these aircraft which crashed within minutes of each other on Horn Cragg, Scafell. The pilots were both Polish airmen serving with the RAF. Much of the wreckage was removed but a search will still reveal some parts of the aircraft.

Date 13 August 1941
Aircraft H Hurricane Mk I R4112 59 OTU
Location Heathergill
Reference 488669
Aircrew Sgt MC Tagseth r62232 RCAF
The pilot was killed and his aircraft destroyed when it crashed near Garahead Farm. The wreckage was removed by a salvage team.

Date 15 August 1941
Aircraft BL Botha Mk I L6354
Location Millom
Reference 103733
Aircrew –
Two miles from RAF Haverigg this aircraft crashed into the sea and sank. Its crew of two were recovered by an air-sea rescue launch from Fleetwood.

The war years

Date 15 August 1941
Aircraft M Magister Mk I T9687 15 EFTS
Location Kingstown
Reference 392594
Aircrew –
This aircraft was badly damaged when it over-shot the runway while landing; its crew were unhurt.

Date 16 August 1941
Aircraft VS Spitfire Mk I X4834 3 FPP
VS Spitfire Mk I X4710 3 FPP
Location Carlisle
Reference 392594
Aircrew –
Following a mid-air collision near Kingstown both pilots managed to land their aircraft on the airfield without further mishap.

Date 16 August 1941
Aircraft M Magister Mk I L8174 15 EFTS
Location Kingstown
Reference 392594
Aircrew –
The undercarriage and wing of this aircraft were badly damaged when an instructor failed to correct a student's heavy landing.

Date 21 August 1941
Aircraft M Magister Mk I V1023
Location Kirkbrampton
Reference 319549
Aircrew Sgt FH Oakley + Air Mec WG Harrow
The pilot and a civilian engine fitter died when this aircraft crashed and collided with a searchlight battery on the Flatts at Kirkbrampton. One report suggests that the aircraft flew down a searchlight beam until it crashed. The wreckage was removed by a salvage unit.

Date 22 August 1941
Aircraft BL Botha Mk I L6416 2 AOS 25 Grp
Location Castle Moss
Reference 875123
Aircrew Sgt W Walisewki, J Yeo 1121315, VJ Humphrey 1058559
The crew of this aircraft lost their lives when it

crashed on Castle Moss near Appleby. Witnesses who saw the crash described how one of the engines ripped itself from the wing of the aircraft shortly before it crashed onto the moss. Most of the wreckage was removed by salvage units, although a few pieces have been located near the site.

Date 24 August 1941
Aircraft M Master Mk I T8739
Location Stapleton
Reference 490700
Aircrew Lft TPG Bastet FFAF
A pilot of the Free French Air Force flying with the RAF died when his aircraft crashed near Kenalhill Farm. The accident occurred as he was approaching Crosby airfield during a night flying exercise. The wreckage was removed by a salvage unit.

Date 25 August 1941
Aircraft H Hurricane Mk I R4099 59 OTU
Location Crosby
Reference 495618
Aircrew Sgt RJ Davies 1058458
After flying over the airfield the aircraft crashed into a small hill at Irthington. The pilot was killed and the aircraft destroyed. The wreckage was removed by a salvage team, but the repaired section of stone wall can still be seen.

Date 25 August 1941
Aircraft M Magister Mk I L8345 15 EFTS
Location Burnfoot
Reference 370660
Aircrew –
This aircraft was badly damaged after it stalled while attempting an emergency landing on the airstrip.

Date 1 September 1941
Aircraft H Hurricane Mk I W9202
Location Dalston
Reference 356489
Aircrew –
A complete engine failure resulted in this aircraft making an emergency landing near Gill Farm at Dalston. Its pilot escaped with minor injuries, but the plane was a total loss and removed later by a salvage unit.

Date 4 September 1941
Aircraft H Hurricane Mk I V6862 59 OTU
Location Penrith
Reference 505325
Aircrew –
A combination of a mechanical failure and poor weather conditions forced the pilot to abandon his aircraft near Penrith. It crashed near the Iron Bridge and Black Barn and was destroyed. The pilot landed safely by parachute a short distance away to be greeted by a number of cows whose attention he had attracted while making his decent. The wreckage was removed by a salvage team a few days later.

Date 5 September 1941
Aircraft VS Spitfire Mk IIa X4622 6 FPP
Location Soulby
Reference 238325
Aircrew H Carter
The same poor weather conditions also caused an ATA pilot to make a forced landing in a field near Soulby, while he was delivering the aircraft to RAF Kirkbride from RAF Coltishall.

When the weather improved, and the slight damage to the aircraft had been repaired, the plane was flown out on the 18th to join 19 Sqd. The serial number attributed to this aircraft is, however, not that of a Spitfire.

Date 8 September 1941
Aircraft H Hector K8096 18 MU
Location Red Pike
Reference 160154
Aircrew F/O JA Craig
Airborne form RAF Binbrook this aircraft crashed into the northern face of Red Pike; it hit a rock outcrop and fell onto a ledge below where it burned out. The location of this crash site made it hard for the rescue teams to reach and recover the pilot's body, and almost all of the wreckage was left on site. The Napier Dagger engine can still be seen today.

Date 9 September 1941
Aircraft H Hurricane Mk I P3880 59 OTU
Location Micklethwaite
Reference 228502
Aircrew Sgt E De-Sapgay

The Free French Air Force pilot of this aircraft was killed after he crashed near Micklethwaite. The wreckage was later removed by a salvage team.

Date 9 September 1941
Aircraft L Hudson Mk I N7337
Location Irish Sea
Reference 000970
Aircrew Cpl RJ Clarke 1051541
No other information is available on this aircraft apart from an official record of its loss in the Irish Sea off Cumberland. Its position was given as mid-way between Seascale and Ramsey.

Date 12 September 1941
Aircraft DH82a Tiger Moth N6723
Location Kingstown
Reference 392546
Aircrew –
The pilot was unhurt following an error in judgement while landing. The aircraft undershot the runway and crashed into a wooden hut and was badly damaged.

Date 12 September 1941
Aircraft H Hurricane Mk I V7251 59 OTU
Location Warwick Bridge
Reference 474558
Aircrew Sgt AML Withers 30334 FFAF
A French pilot was killed and his aircraft destroyed when it crashed near Low Wood Farm. People who saw the accident reported that the aircraft came straight down from a height of around five thousand feet. The wreckage was removed by a salvage unit.

Date 17 September 1941
Aircraft M Magister Mk I L8073 15 EFTS
51 Grp
Location Lowther Park
Reference 508212
Aircrew –
Having been reported overdue by the officer commanding RAF Crosby, a large-scale search was undertaken to locate the aircraft. An ARP observer reported seeing the aircraft flying south towards Lowther at 200 feet during the afternoon and the search was concentrated in that area. The

plane was found in Lowther Park later that day; it had crashed into the ground and exploded killing its pilot and causing a large crater. The wreckage was removed later by a salvage unit.

Date	17 September 1941
Aircraft	DH Tiger Moth Mk II T6498
	15 EFTS
	M Magister Mk I N5432 15 EFTS
Location	Kingstown
Reference	392594
Aircrew	–

Having landed a Magister too close to the Tiger Moth it crashed into it causing severe damage to both aircraft. Its crew were unhurt. The Tiger Moth was destroyed in an accident in July 1943.

Date	18 September 1941
Aircraft	H Hurricane Mk II V6998 59 OTU
Location	Crosby
Reference	480605
Aircrew	W/Cdr DPH Boitel-Gill 28142

A decorated and distinguished pilot died in this accident. The aircraft flew low across the runway and crashed near the petrol dump where it burned out.

Date	20 September 1941
Aircraft	M Magister Mk I T7740 15 EFTS
Location	Longtown
Reference	420683
Aircrew	–

This Magister crashed near Longtown airfield while on a training flight. Its crew were unhurt and the aircraft was removed by a salvage team.

Date	20 September 1941
Aircraft	F Battle P2181
Location	Kelsic
Reference	184504
Aircrew	–

The pilot of this aircraft made a crash-landing in a field near Kelsic; he was unhurt and the aircraft was later removed on a low loader.

Date	21 September 1941
Aircraft	H Hurricane Mk I P3623 59 OTU
Location	Westlinton
Reference	409645
Aircrew	Sgt W Brownlie NZ405227

Salvage units removed the wreckage of this aircraft a short time after it crashed killing its pilot at Westlinton. Wreckage was scattered over a wide area.

Date	22 September 1941
Aircraft	M Magister Mk I L8055
	15 EFTS
	M Magister Mk I L8337
	15 EFTS
Location	Kingstown
Reference	392259
Aircrew	–

Two accidents at RAF Kingstown. One aircraft crashed on the airfield after its undercarriage collapsed, due to its being damaged earlier when the pilot hit the surface of the water while low flying.

The second aircraft made a heavy landing, bounced, then its undercarriage collapsed when it came into contact with the ground again. Both aircraft were recovered by crash teams.

Date	25 September 1941
Aircraft	B Botha Mk I L6277
Location	Millom
Reference	140790
Aircrew	–

Few details on this accident are available other than the report of it crashing on take-off at RAF Haverigg.

Date	27 September 1941
Aircraft	HP Hampden
Location	Millom
Reference	140790
Aircrew	–

After the pilot failed to notice a warning light, the tail wheel of this aircraft collapsed as it was taxiing. The aircraft swung off the runway, causing a considerable amount of damage to the under surfaces of the tail section.

Date	29 September 1941
Aircraft	M Master Mk III W8594
Location	Bewcastle .
Reference	615790
Aircrew	Sgt GF Hillier NZ402445

While on ATA transport duties, a New Zealand

pilot serving with the RAF was delivering the aircraft to the Central Flying School when his aircraft crashed on Tarn Beck Fell. He was killed and his aircraft destroyed. Wreckage of this aircraft was recovered by salvage teams using horses and sledges.

Date	1 October 1941
Aircraft	A Oxford Mk IV
Location	Rockcliff
Reference	370630
Aircrew	P/O RA McAnney.
	Sgt JG Wallace 653005

The crew of this aircraft were killed after it crashed between Rockcliff and Todhills. The wreckage was removed later by salvage units.

Date	4 October 1941
Aircraft	VS Spitfire Vb AB987
Location	Kirkbride
Reference	230550
Aircrew	–

This aircraft overshot the runway while landing and overturned. The pilot escaped unhurt and reported the cause of the accident as being his forgetting to lower the aircraft flaps.

Date	10 October 1941
Aircraft	B Beaufighter Mk If T4797
Location	Silloth
Reference	126542
Aircrew	–

After landing on a flooded runway, the aircraft swung off and ran into soft ground where it overturned. The crew escaped without serious injury and the aircraft was salvaged and returned into service following repair.

Date	16 October 1941
Aircraft	BL Botha Mk I L6425 2 AOS
	25 Grp
Location	Ravenglass
Reference	112949
Aircrew	–

The crew of this aircraft escaped with only minor injuries when the aircraft crashed into Broad Quarry following an engine failure.

Date	20 October 1941
Aircraft	HP Hampden Mk I P2127
	12 MU
Location	Westfield
Reference	258549
Aircrew	Sgt A Raw 748237, Civilian A Robson

A civilian engine fitter and the pilot of this aircraft were killed as the plane crashed at Westfield near Little Brampton. The aircraft was being flown on an air test when the accident occurred. The wreckage was removed by a crash recovery team.

Date	20 October 1941
Aircraft	VS Spitfire Mk IIa P7678
Location	Kirkbride
Reference	230550
Aircrew	–

An ATA pilot forgot to lower his undercarriage while landing on the airfield. Although he escaped uninjured, the plane was badly damaged.

Date	27 October 1941
Aircraft	Unknown
Location	Hoff
Reference	640190
Aircrew	–

A police report exists of an unidentified aircraft making an emergency landing in a field, close to the King's Meaburn to Hoff road due to a fuel shortage at 1343 hrs. The pilot obtained fuel locally, refuelled his aircraft and flew away.

Date	28 October 1941
Aircraft	H Hurricane Mk I V7236 59 OTU
Location	Kingstown
Reference	397598
Aircrew	Sgt SD Fassino r84013

The pilot of this aircraft was killed after he flew into trees at Greymore Hill near Kingstown airfield. Salvage units had to recover wreckage from a wide area and from amidst the branches of the trees.

Date 2 November 1941
Aircraft A Oxford Mk I AT486
Location Caw Fell
Reference 125106
Aircrew Sgt CA Des-Baillets r79007,
RCAF Sgt Hodkinson
Remains of this aircraft can still be located at its crash site at Red Cragg on Caw Fell. Its crew were killed in the impact and an area blackened by the intense fire can still be seen. Many remains are buried at the crash site.

Date 2 November 1941
Aircraft M Magister Mk I N3840 15 EFTS
Location Kingstown
Reference –
Aircrew –
The pilot of this aircraft made a heavy landing the plane bounced, stalled and then crashed down onto the airfield. The crew were unhurt and the plane was removed by a crash team.

Date 5 November 1941
Aircraft M Magister Mk I L5925
M Magister Mk I T9948
Location Kingstown
Reference 392259
Aircrew –
Both of these aircraft were badly damaged after the first landed and then crashed into the second. Ground mechanics pulled the aircraft apart and found the crew were unhurt.

Date 8 November 1941
Aircraft M Magister Mk I L5988 15 EFTS
Location Kingstown
Reference 392259
Aircrew –
This aircraft was only slightly damaged after its pilot made an emergency landing in deteriorating weather. The pilot was unhurt and the aircraft was repaired a short time later.

Date 8 November 1941
Aircraft M Magister Mk I N3779 5 EFTS
Location Carlisle
Reference 392594
Aircrew –
Another forced landing on this day, in rough pas-

ture near Kingstown. The aircraft was slightly damaged and its pilot unhurt.

Date 10 November 1941
Aircraft H Hurricane Mk I W9342 59 OTU
Location Westnewton
Reference 157446
Aircrew –
The pilot of this aircraft was killed after it crashed near Crossrigg Farm, Westnewton. The wreckage was later removed by a crash unit.

Date 11 November 1941
Aircraft H Hurricane Mk I R4080 59 OTU
Location Westlinton
Reference 389638
Aircrew Sgt JW Moreux 30597 FFAF
The Free French Air Force pilot of this aircraft was killed after he crashed into a small field near Westlinton village. The wreckage was removed later by a salvage team.

Date 12 November 1941
Aircraft DH Tiger Moth Mk II T6497
15 EFTS
Location Kingstown
Reference 392259
Aircrew –
After stalling while landing the aircraft crashed down onto the airfield and was badly damaged. The pilot was unhurt.

Date 13 November 1941
Aircraft M Magister Mk I N3987 15 EFTS
M Magister Mk I V1097 15 EFTS
Location Kingstown
Reference 392259
Aircrew –
Both aircraft were damaged after the pilot of N3987 landed too close to the other and crashed into it. The crew were unhurt.

Date 14 November 1941
Aircraft L Hudson Mk V AM536
Location Solway Firth
Reference 135593
Aircrew Sgt JA Stark 1365119, Sgt F Prine 961793, Sgt JM Holson 953386
The crew of this aircraft were killed after it

crashed into the Solway Firth, it broke up and sank very quickly.

Date 15 November 1941
Aircraft B Airacobra Mk I AH598 3 FPP
Location Kirkbride
Reference 256572
Aircrew Cpt W Handley
The pilot of this aircraft was the Commanding Officer of No 3 Ferry pool at RAF Harwarden, and was also a famous TT motorcycle rider. He had taken off from Harwarden in an Anson for RAF Kirkbride, once there he collected a 'chit' to take an Airacobra back to Harwarden. A few minutes after take-off thick black smoke was seen coming from the aircraft's engine and there was a loud explosion followed by a sheet of flame which engulfed the rear of the aircraft. Part of the aircraft was seen to break off and it turned to an angle of forty-five degrees. It crashed near Fingland killing its pilot. An accident investigation later proved that the engine had been overboosted and over-revved during the take-off run.

Date 17 November 1941
Aircraft M Magister Mk I N5432
15 EFTS
M Magister Mk I R1855
15 EFTS
Location Kingstown
Reference 392594
Aircrew –
Another airfield accident caused by N5432 landing too close to and crashing into R1855.

Date 19 November 1941
Aircraft A Oxford Mk I AT478 2 AOS
Location Wigton
Reference 246409
Aircrew P/O RAL White, LAC EE
Clandage 1375671, LAC SH
Bingham 1208877
The crew of three died when this aircraft crashed and disintegrated upon impact on Gatlands Fell. The crash occurred in poor visibility and driving rain. Salvage teams had to rake the field to remove the remains of the aircraft.

Date 19 November 1941
Aircraft HP Hampden Mk I L4076
Location Kirkbride
Reference 230550
Aircrew –
The crew of this aircraft escaped unhurt after the undercarriage failed during take-off.

Date 22 November 1941
Aircraft M Magister Mk I L8174 15 EFTS
Location Kingstown
Reference 392594
Aircrew –
This aircraft crashed at the end of the runway. The cause turned out to be the pilot trying to take-off on a training flight with no fuel in the aircraft's tanks.

Date 25 November 1941
Aircraft H Hurricane Mk I T9524
59 OTU
Location Brampton
Reference 543676
Aircrew –
The pilot of this aircraft escaped without serious injury after he crashed his aircraft into Nickies Hill near Brampton. The wreckage was removed later by a salvage team.

Date 25 November 1941
Aircraft M Magister Mk 14a T9973
15 EFTS
Location Kingstown
Reference 392594
Aircrew –
During a training flight the pilot's parachute slipped forward jamming the control column. A recovery was made but the aircraft crashed on the airfield.

Date 27 November 1941
Aircraft VS Spitfire Mk Vb VL412
Location Kirkbride
Reference 230550
Aircrew –
An ATA pilot escaped with only minor injuries after he overshot the runway and overturned in strong winds.

Date 27 November 1941
Aircraft H Hurricane Mk I P3228
59 OTU
Location Harker
Reference 387614
Aircrew –
This pilot was taken to a local hospital for treatment after his aircraft crashed near Harker Station, north of Carlisle. The wreckage was removed by a salvage team.

Date 28 November 1941
Aircraft B Botha Mk I W5053
No 2 B &G School
Location Millom
Reference 137804
Aircrew Sgt JR Jones 655191,
AC2 E Clark 112052
LAC EH Jump 1335202,
LAC Reid 1385614
Shortly after taking off the aircraft crashed and burned out near Layriggs Farm. Its crew died in the accident and the wreckage was removed later by a salvage unit.

Date 28 November 1941
Aircraft M Magister Mk I T9871
15 EFTS
Location Kingstown
Reference 392594
Aircrew –
This aircraft was badly damaged after the pilot taxied too fast downwind and overturned. He escaped unhurt.

Date 28 November 1941
Aircraft DH Dominie 89a X7402
Location Derwentwater
Reference 267215
Aircrew Sgt CGA Tarbor 1651995,
LAC JCB Hards 657558,
LAC RF Griffen 1338278,
LAC L Morries 1501436
According to witnesses of this accident, the aircraft flew low over the lake in good weather conditions and with good visibility when it then crashed into the water. None of the crew escaped before it sank. Salvage teams worked with a local boat company to recover the wreckage

from the bed of the lake, after which it was removed for examination.

Date 29 November 1941
Aircraft W Lysander Mk IIIa V9589
15 EFTS
H Henley L3254 15 EFTS
Location Kingstown
Reference 392594
Aircrew –
Both aircraft were damaged after the Henley overshot the runway and crashed into the parked Lysander.

Date 1 December 1941
Aircraft H Hector K9729
Location Millom
Reference 140790
Aircrew –
The pilot of this aircraft made a crash-landing on the airfield at RAF Haverigg following an engine failure. The aircraft was wrecked but the pilot escaped with only minor injuries.

Date 3 December 1941
Aircraft H Hurricane Mk I AF985
Location Mawbray
Reference 119569
Aircrew Sqd Ldr TG Pace 39243
A test pilot flying this aircraft was killed when he crashed into the Solway Firth. Local people who saw the accident say that the aircraft came straight down from a considerable height.

Date 8 December 1941
Aircraft Horsa Glider
Location Arnside
Reference 456769
Aircrew –
A troop-carrying glider was being towed from Dumfries to Ringway when it parted company with its tug following a cable break. The crew made an emergency landing close to Arnside tower; they were unhurt and a police guard was posted on the glider until it was recovered

Date 10 December 1941
Aircraft H Hurricane Mk I W9342 59 OTU
Location Westnewton
Reference 155448
Aircrew –
On a training flight from Crosby, this aircraft crashed killing its pilot near to Crossrigg Farm. The wreckage was removed a short time later.

Date 13 December 1941
Aircraft P Proctor P28 Mk III R7537
Location Millom
Reference 140790
Aircrew –
Being taxied by an ATA pilot this aircraft was caught in a strong crosswind and overturned. The aircraft was badly damaged but the pilot was unhurt.

Date 14 December 1941
Aircraft D Boston, Mk III Z2299
Location Kendal
Reference 478893
Aircrew F/O JF Wolfe
A combination of low fuel and poor weather conditions caused this pilot to make a forced landing in a field near Brigsteer. After touching down the aircraft ran into soft ground and the nose wheel was ripped off causing the aircraft to flop onto its belly. The pilot was unhurt and the aircraft was later dismantled and removed by road on low loaders. The drivers had problems reaching the crash site because of the narrow roads in the area.

Date 14 December 1941
Aircraft L Hudson Mk I N7223
Location Silloth
Reference 126542
Aircrew Sgt AJ Birchwood 1060440
This aircraft crashed on the airfield killing its pilot; recovery teams later removed the wreckage.

Date 15 December 1941
Aircraft H Hector K9760
Location Millom
Reference 140790
Aircrew –
An engine failure on take-off caused the aircraft to crash into a small field at the end of the runway at RAF Haverigg.

Date 17 December 1941
Aircraft A Anson Mk I N9842
Location Millom
Reference 134802
Aircrew Sgt WM Pepper J8618,
Sgt A Gibbons 1000983,
Sgt W Peggie r60617
Local people reported that this aircraft was on fire as it crashed into the sea off Millom. One crew member was saved by a local boatman who fished him out of the water. Remains of the aircraft are buried in the sand and the aircraft's engine can still be seen from time to time at low tide when the sands shift.

Date 19 December 1941
Aircraft M Master Mk III W8479
Location Sedbergh
Reference 650970
Aircrew –
A Polish ATA pilot was killed after he flew into a fellside two and a half miles north of Sedbergh. His body was recovered but the majority of the aircraft was left on site. Unfortunately no accurate record of its location was kept and the best location to date has been White Fell. A number of searches have been made in this area but the remains have not yet been located.

Date 19 December 1941
Aircraft HP Hampden Mk I L4076
Location Kirkbride
Reference 230550
Aircrew P/O J Marrey
The crew of this aircraft escaped unhurt after its undercarriage collapsed during its take-off run.

Date 20 December 1941
Aircraft H Hurricane Mk I R4086 59 OTU
H Hurricane Mk I V7601 50 OTU
Location Irthington
Reference 493005
Aircrew Sgt KF Peters RCAF r95372,
P/O DF Meachann 111702
It is believed that these aircraft were involved in a mid-air collision before they crashed near Irthington killing their pilots. The wreckage was removed by salvage teams.

Date 21 December 1941
Aircraft VS Spitfire Mk I X4059
Location Kirkbride
Reference 140790
Aircrew –
This aircraft ran off the runway while taking off and overturned in soft ground. The pilot was uninjured and the aircraft was later repaired on site, and then returned into service.

Date 21 December 1941
Aircraft L Hudson Mk V AM624 1c OTU
Location Dent Fell
Reference 702854
Aircrew Sgt ED Parrish r77526
This aircraft was seen flying low with its engine and fuselage in flames. It crashed on Dent Fell and exploded killing its crew and spreading wreckage over a wide area. The majority of the wreckage was buried at the crash site in a shallow pit, although this is difficult to find now as a small plantation has grown over the crash site.

Date 28 December 1941
Aircraft L Hudson Mk V AM786 1c OTU
Location Maryport
Reference 057368
Aircrew RW Allsop Aus402455, GI
Backhouse 400487, Sgt H Punsepp
40252, H Rissopp 40252,
Sgt RG Luke Aus400722
The crew of this aircraft died after it cartwheeled and exploded while trying to make a forced landing at Haybrough. The wreckage was removed by salvage teams.

Date 29 December 1941
Aircraft Wellington (unconfirmed)
Location Fisher Tarn
Reference 556925
Aircrew –
This aircraft remains unidentified. It crashed onto a main road and then into a small hill near the Old Gin Shop after jettisoning its bomb load. Some of these bombs had to be recovered from a local reservoir. The aircraft is thought to have been a Wellington bomber, which was destroyed in the crash.

Date 1 January 1942
Aircraft BP Defiant Mk I N3432 96 Sqd
Location Troutbeck
Reference 430038
Aircrew Sgt H Wolfe rYY476
Wreckage from this aircraft can still be found on the fellside above the Old Quarry at Troutbeck. It crashed shortly after two in the afternoon in poor weather conditions flying from RAF East Fortune. The aircraft hit a stone wall running along the top of the fell, causing it to explode and catapult down the opposite side. Many large parts, including the gear reduction unit and even the pilot's flare pistol, have been found at this site. In recent years the site has been excavated and many parts removed.

Date 4 January 1942
Aircraft V Wellington Mk II W5389
HP Hampden
Location Kirkbride
Reference 230550
Aircrew –
After landing on the wrong runway the aircraft was caught in a strong crosswind; it swung off the runway and into a parked Hampden bomber.

Date 9 January 1942
Aircraft H Hurricane
Location Dufton Fell
Reference 705256
Aircrew P/O Amos
An engine failure caused the pilot to make a forced landing at Fawcett Park. The aircraft was repaired on site and flown out the following day. The station log records the incident and the pilot, but not the aircraft's identity.

Date 9 January 1942
Aircraft M Magister Mk I N3936
15 EFTS
Location Carlisle
Reference 392259
Aircrew –
This aircraft made a forced landing in a small field near Kingstown airfield following an engine failure. It was removed by a salvage team.

Date 9 January 1942
Aircraft M Magister Mk I L5935 15 EFTS
Location Kingstown
Reference 392594
Aircrew –
An engine failure caused this aircraft to crash-land on the airfield. The pilot was unhurt but the plane was badly damaged.

Date 9 January 1942
Aircraft P Proctor Mk I R7491
VS Spitfire W3569
Location Kirkbride
Reference 230550
Aircrew –
Taxying on the runway, this aircraft swerved to avoid a Spitfire which landed over the top of the Proctor. The Proctor ran into a ditch and was severely damaged.

Date 10 January 1942
Aircraft B Beaufighter Mk If T4884
HP Hampden
Location Kirkbride
Reference 230550
Aircrew –

This aircraft's brakes jammed on while taxying down the runway. It swung off and crashed into a parked Hampden bomber.

Date 10 January 1942
Aircraft A Anson (536)
Location Millom
Reference 109801
Aircrew Sgt MH Wadham 407740,
L Gibson 400467
The crew of this aircraft died after it crashed into the sea off Silecroft. The plane broke up and sank quickly, its crew of two were unable to escape. The only identification given for this aircraft was its wing number. The body of one crew member was not recovered until June that year.

Date 10 January 1942
Aircraft HP Hampden Mk I AE250 50 Sqd
Location Brampton
Reference 519618
Aircrew Sgt S Earnshaw 92660,
Sgt AR Bernard 1004002,
Sgt LC Williams 1377183
This aircraft crashed killing its crew near

Part of the Defiant's gear reduction unit found above Troutbeck. The identity plate assisted in confirming the aircraft's identity. (MJ Hurst)

Brampton. No other information is available on the incident.

Date 13 January 1942
Aircraft M Magister Mk I P2468
Location Carlisle
Reference 379551
Aircrew –

Flying from RAF Sealand to RAF Kingstown the pilot encountered poor weather. He was advised to fly to RAF Haverigg but he ignored this advice and continued. He crashed the aircraft near Carlisle at Raffels. The aircraft was a total loss but its pilot escaped with minor injuries.

Date 17 January 1942
Aircraft M Magister Mk I R1849 15 EFTS
Location Carlisle
Reference 392594
Aircrew –

After becoming lost in poor weather the pilot made a forced landing near Carlisle. The aircraft was removed by a salvage unit.

Date 19 January 1942
Aircraft H Hurricane (Z9)
Location Fawcett Park
Reference 707248
Aircrew Pilot Woodcock

Recorded in the station diary as aircraft Z9, a mechanical failure caused the pilot to make a landing in a snow-covered field above Appleby. The aircraft remained on site until it was recovered on the 26th.

Date 28 January 1942
Aircraft M Magister Mk I L5928 15 EFTS
Location Rockcliff
Reference 351620
Aircrew Sgt B Astley Aus403422 RAAF

The pilot of this aircraft was killed as he crashed on the drive of Castletown House. Help was quickly on the scene but little could be done. The wreckage was removed by a salvage unit.

Date 28 January 1942
Aircraft M Master Mk I T8614 12 Grp
Location Stainmoor
Reference 892138
Aircrew Section Officer RH Winn 114467

An ATA pilot flying from Dumfries to RAF Caterick crashed at Beldoo Hill. He was killed in the accident but remained undiscovered until 4 April. A visit to this site will still show wreckage from the aircraft.

Date 31 January 1942
Aircraft L Hudson Mk I T9308 1c OTU
Location Great Corby
Reference 482540
Aircrew P/O DMC Burgess J5913 RCAF, Sgt JRV Barnes 1168

Two crew were killed when this plane crashed near Great Corby village and burst into flames. The wreckage was later removed by a salvage team.

Date 1 February 1942
Aircraft H Hurricane Mk I Z4575 55 OTU
Location Kingstown
Reference 392594
Aircrew –

An engine failure caused this crash-landing on the airfield. The crew were unhurt and the aircraft was removed by a crash team.

Date 6 February 1942
Aircraft H Hurricane Mk I L1638
Location Kirkbride
Reference 230550
Aircrew –

The ATA pilot of this aircraft was badly injured when it crashed near the airfield. The accident occurred in poor weather during a flight from Rearsly to RAF Silloth where it was due to enter service.

Date 8 February 1942
Aircraft V Wellington T2714 22 OTU
Location Skiddaw
Reference 286330
Aircrew EG Jenner r78631, DJ Richardson j6134, F/Sgt LJ Raymond BE Chard

During a training flight from its base at RAF Wellesbourne, the aircraft crashed on a Sunday killing its crew. The scree slopes and gill above Brun Todd still hold many parts from the aircraft.

Date   8 February 1942
Aircraft   A Anson Mk I W1793
Location   Stainmoor
Reference   841119
Aircrew   Pilot WJ Elliot
En route from RAF Sherburn in Emlet to RAF Kirkbride, this aircraft crashed onto Buckles Heath, South Stainmoor killing its pilot. The plane was destroyed and some of the wreckage removed by a salvage unit. An enquiry found that the aircraft crashed into the snow line on the fell side. It was felt that the snow line may have been mistaken for the cloud base.

Date   12 February 1942
Aircraft   W Lysander Mk III P9125
Location   Kirkbride
Reference   230550
Aircrew   –
This aircraft was overturned by a strong gust of wind after it landed on the wrong runway. Although the aircraft was badly damaged, its ATA pilot was unhurt.

Date   14 February 1942
Aircraft   VS Spitfire Mk Vb BL898
Location   Kirkbride
Reference   230550
Aircrew   –
An ATA pilot made an error when he did not lower the flaps on the aircraft; this caused the aircraft to overshoot the runway and crash near the perimeter.

Date   16 February 1942
Aircraft   BP Defiant Mk TT III N1764
Location   Great Orton
Reference   313586
Aircrew   –
Poor weather and low fuel prompted the pilot to make an emergency landing on a satellite airfield which was under construction at Great Orton. Because of the many obstructions on the airfield the pilot had difficulty in landing, and while trying to avoid one of them he crashed. The pilot was unhurt and the aircraft recovered later.

Date   16 February 1942
Aircraft   HP Halifax Mk II L9619 10 Sqd
                4 Grp
Location   Keld
Reference   500130
Aircrew   F/Sgt Lloyd, P/O Hillier,
                Sgt Mapes, F/Sgt Guertin
                Sgt Mathias Sgt Thain Sgt Gifford
Returning from a raid on St Nazaire, this aircraft became lost and began to run low on fuel; the order to bale out was given near Appleby and the crew landed safely. Meanwhile the aircraft continued until it crashed just south of Keld in the Ralfland Forest area of Westmorland. This aircraft did not have the usual mid upper turret. Certainly wreckage has been found in this area, but some sites are quite removed from each other, giving rise to a theory of there being more than one aircraft in the locality.

Date   18 February 1942
Aircraft   L Hudson Mk V AM825
Location   Solway Firth
Reference   041461
Aircrew   P/O TR Godfrey j6171 RCAF,
                Sgt JF Green 1112439,
                D Thomas 916123, 1 ANO
After leaving the airfield at ten thirty in the evening, reports of an aircraft crashing into the Solway Firth began to arrive at the control centre around eleven p.m. Reports later confirmed that it had crashed into the sea off Dubmill Point killing its crew. On occasions parts are washed up on the beaches in this area. However, as many aircraft were lost in this vicinity one cannot be sure which aircraft they are from.

Date   23 February 1942
Aircraft   A Anson Mk I AX565
                DH 89 Dominie Mk I Z7256
Location   Millom
Reference   140790
Aircrew   Sgt JDD White R85735
Following a mid-air collision these aircraft crashed onto Haverigg airfield. One crewman from the Anson survived the accident. The wreckage was later removed by salvage units.

Date 23 February 1942
Aircraft VS Spitfire R7173
Location Kirkbride
Reference 230550
Aircrew Sgt Duncan FFP
During a ferry flight the pilot landed at Kirkbride, hitting an obstruction. The pilot was unhurt but the aircraft was badly damaged.

Date 12 March 1942
Aircraft A Oxford Mk II X7185
Location Kirkbride
Reference 230550
Aircrew –
After being hit by a crosswind the pilot lost control and the plane swung from the runway, its undercarriage collapsed and it dropped onto its port wing. The crew were unhurt.

Date 15 March 1942
Aircraft L Hudson Mk V AM774
Location Kirkbride
Reference 230550
Aircrew –

This crew were unhurt after their aircraft overshot the runway and crashed into obstructions beyond.

Date 25 March 1942
Aircraft L Hudson Mk 1 N7392
Location Solway Firth
Reference 087572
Aircrew Sgt MC Taylor 403452
W/O G Essan 405151 RAAF
Another evening training flight from Silloth and another aircraft lost in the Firth. The crew and rescue teams managed to recover only one body.

Date 26 March 1942
Aircraft M Magister Mk I N3830
15 EFTS
Location Kingstown
Reference 392594
Aircrew –
An engine failure on take-off caused the pilot to crash at the end of the runway. He was unhurt but the plane was badly damaged.

Halifax Bomber L9619. (Imperial War Museum, London)

Date 27 March 1942
Aircraft H Hurricane Mk II Z3401
Location Silloth
Reference 126542
Aircrew F/O Newmark

Attempting to take-off on the wrong runway this plane collided with a second aircraft; both were badly damaged.

Date 28 March 1942
Aircraft M Magister Mk I R1959 15 EFTS
Location Kingstown
Reference 392594
Aircrew –

A heavy landing during a night flying exercise caused the undercarriage to collapse. The aircraft was badly damaged but its pilot was unhurt.

Date 4 April 1942
Aircraft Unknown
Location Witherslack
Reference 433845
Aircrew –

The following police report records this incident, but not the aircraft type or its serial number.

A middle-aged man and teenager from Lancaster were each fined ten shillings for trespassing without reasonable excuse on agricultural land, and doing damage to corn to the extent of ten shillings. The offences were committed when the men went to look at an RAF machine which came down in a field near Witherslack. PC X said he was on duty in Methop Lane preventing people from entering the fields of growing corn where the aircraft had landed. Mr Y advised the court that he was the owner of the field.

Date 11 April 1942
Aircraft Unidentified
Location Seascale
Reference 040900
Aircrew –

An unidentified aircraft was seen to ditch into the sea off Seascale and sink. It has not yet been located or its identity traced.

Date 13 April 1942
Aircraft H Hurricane Mk I Z7150 59 OTU
81 Grp
H Hurricane Mk I Z4103 59 OTU
81 Grp
Location Kirkbride
Reference 230550
Aircrew Pilot Sgt BW Taylor RCAF
r90503 + ANO

Following a mid-air collision one aircraft crashed a mile south of the airfield killing its pilot. The second aircraft managed to return to the airfield and made a high-speed crash-landing. The accident occurred in poor weather conditions.

Date 13 April 1942
Aircraft L Hudson 1c OTU
Location Kirkbride
Reference 030550
Aircrew –

After landing on the airfield the aircraft overshot, crashed through a fence and ran into a civilian lorry. Both were badly damaged.

Date 27 April 1942
Aircraft P Proctor P34 Mk III DX225
Location Kirkbride
Reference 230550
Aircrew –

Trying to taxi the aircraft in strong winds resulted in the pilot losing control and the aircraft overturned. Its pilot was unhurt and the aircraft later repaired on site.

Date 7 May 1942
Aircraft A Anson Mk I R9757
Location Millom
Reference 140790
Aircrew –

During an ATA delivery flight the pilot made a forced landing on Haverigg airfield. The cause was a complete failure of the port engine. The aircraft was repaired on site and returned into service.

Date 7 May 1942
Aircraft H Hurricane Mk I P3116
59 OTU 81 Grp
Location Penton
Reference Unconfirmed
Aircrew Sgt VT Wolfe R83292
While carrying out some very low flying this aircraft crashed into Kingsfield House at Penton. The pilot was killed along with an occupant in the house. Six months before the aircraft had crashed at Jedburgh, it had been salvaged, repaired and returned into service.

Date 10 May 1942
Aircraft V Wellington Mk III Z1722
Location Millom
Reference 140790
Aircrew –
Faulty oil pipes and leaks after an engine failure caused an emergency landing at Haverigg airfield. Repairs were carried out on site and the aircraft returned into service.

Date 19 May 1942
Aircraft B Botha Mk I W5051
Location Wigton
Reference 209508
Aircrew –
One crew member was injured after the aircraft crashed while taking off from a satellite airfield at Wathead; the aircraft sustained medium damage.

Date 24 May 1942
Aircraft L Hudson Mk V AM794
Location Millom
Reference 179777
Aircraft F/O RW Rollalson 403018
A few minutes after taking off from Haverigg airfield this aircraft crashed into the sea and sank. Its crew were killed and the pilot's body was recovered on 24 June.

Date 26 May 1942
Aircraft M Master Mk I N7884
Location Wreay
Reference 443488
Aircrew Sgt GE Barden 1292442,
Sgt RA Way R98787
The crew died after this aircraft struck the tops

of some trees and crashed near Wreay Hall. The pilot had been low flying in the area prior to the accident. The burnt out remains were removed by a salvage unit.

Date 5 June 1942
Aircraft H Hurricane (MF) 601 Sqd
Location Appleby
Reference 704157
Aircrew –
The pilot of this aircraft was killed while low flying when he crashed into the ground near Helm Farm Wood.

Date 6 June 1942
Aircraft HP Halifax Mk II W7668 78 Sqd
4 Grp
Location Methop
Reference 443822
Aircrew W/Cdr Lucas, P/O Ide,
Sgt Frankland, Sgt Davies,
Sgt Seal, Sgt Smith, Sgt Williams
Returning from a bombing raid on Bremen to its base at RAF Croft, a fuel shortage prompted the pilot to make a forced landing in a field at the side of the main road at Methop. The crew escaped with minor injuries but the aircraft was badly damaged and later removed by road on a low loader.

Date 9 June 1942
Aircraft L Hudson Mk I N7307
Location Silloth
Reference 126542
Aircrew Sgt EA Jefferson 137645,
Sgt DH Shirley 167939
The crew of this Hudson lost their lives after the aircraft crashed down on the runway during take-off, and erupted in flames almost at once. Salvage and rescue teams removed the wreckage.

Date 11 June 1942
Aircraft M Magister Mk I R1851
15 EFTS
Location Dalston
Reference 364511
Aircrew P/O J Bramely 116574, WL Webb
1686919 (6sm53)
Nothing remains to mark the impact point where

this aircraft crashed close to Forrest House killing its crew. The remains were removed by a salvage unit.

Date	15 June 1941
Aircraft	H Hurricane Mk I W9217 55 OTU
Location	Crofton
Reference	304496
Aircrew	–

This aircraft made a crash-landing in a field at East Park near Crofton Hall. The aircraft provided a lot of interest for local people until it was recovered.

Date	15 June 1942
Aircraft	H Hurricane
Location	Kirkbride
Reference	230550
Aircrew	–

An undercarriage failure caused the crash-landing of this aircraft on the airfield; its identity was not recorded.

Date	16 June 1942
Aircraft	DH Tiger Moth Mk II T6812
Location	Carlisle
Reference	390595
Aircrew	Sgt GD Weir 978010

After crashing near Kingstown airfield, the aircraft burst into flames killing its RAFVR instructor pilot, the wreckage was removed by a salvage team.

Date	20 June 1942
Aircraft	M Magister
Location	Appleby
Reference	669274
Aircrew	–

Flying from Derby to Kingstown a fuel shortage caused the pilot to make a forced landing on Knock Moor. The pilot telephoned his position to Carlisle and a short time later a Tiger Moth arrived with extra fuel. Once refuelled they left for Crosby.

Date	23 June 1942
Aircraft	H Hurricane Mk I V7001
	59 OTU 81 Grp
Location	Dovenby
Reference	090337
Aircrew	Sgt Much

The pilot was killed as the aircraft crashed near Dovenby, the wreckage was removed by a salvage unit. The aircraft's record card shows that it was converted to a Sea Hurricane.

Date	25 June 1942
Aircraft	H Hurricane Mk I N2666
	55 OTU 81 Grp
Location	Easton
Reference	425729
Aircrew	Sgt S Allcock RNAF 33973

After carrying out a low flying exercise on the gunnery range, the aircraft crashed in a field at Fingland Moss near Easton village killing its pilot. Wreckage was scattered over a wide area and removed by a salvage team.

Date	26 June 1942
Aircraft	H Hurricane Mk I P2877 59 OTU
	81 Grp
Location	Black How, Cleator
Reference	025134
Aircrew	Sgt B Nicholls 610074

This aircraft was seen to go out of control while flying in formation with two more Hurricanes, it crashed near Black How Farm, Cleator killing its pilot. The engine had to be pulled from the crater by a tractor when crash teams were recovering the wreckage.

Date	5 July 1942
Aircraft	H Hurricane Mk I BW481
Location	Millom
Reference	140790
Aircrew	–

Having undershot the runway the aircraft's undercarriage collapsed, and the aircraft crashed onto its wing. It was recovered by a crash team. The serial number of this aircraft was not allocated to a Hurricane, hence identification is uncertain.

Date	5 July 1942
Aircraft	H Hurricane Mk I P2684 601 Sqd
Location	Appleby
Reference	715158
Aircrew	LD Rymoer

After making a number of low passes in the area, the plane struck the top of some trees at Helm

Farm Wood, cartwheeled into the ground and burst into flames. The pilot was killed and little remained of the aircraft. Though much of the aircraft was removed at the time, some fragments have been found in the woods.

Date 7 July 1942
Aircraft M Master Mk I T8411 55OTU
Location Kelsick
Reference 278585
Aircrew Sgt J Tresiter 412287 RNZAF, F/Lt Rockwell

This aircraft was on air test from the satellite landing ground at Longtown. The instructor had agreed to carry out a flight training check on a Sergeant pilot who had crash-landed two Hurricane fighters the same day. The Sergeant had requested a dual check with the instructor. During the flight, a wing was seen to break off the aircraft during a spin. As the aircraft began to break up, the instructor told the student to bale out. The instructor was able to escape but the student was unable to free himself and was killed as the aircraft crashed near Wedholme Farm. The wreckage of the aircraft impacted deep into the soft ground and crash teams were unable to recover the body of the pilot because of water filling the excavation. The crash investigation revealed that the aircraft had been involved in two previous accidents and the cause was thought to have been structural failure. Much of the wreckage was left at the crash site.

Date 8 July 1942
Aircraft H Hurricane Mk I AG125 55 OTU
Location Easton
Reference 278587
Aircrew Sgt AL Gane NZ1375959

A New Zealand pilot serving with the RAF was killed when his aircraft crashed and exploded near Easton. Salvage units removed the wreckage a few days later.

Date 8 July 1942
Aircraft H Hurricane Mk I Z7077 55 OTU
Location Solway
Reference 268611
Aircrew Sgt TR Robieson 1375959

Very little information is available regarding this accident other than a record of it crashing into the sands off Drumburgh. The pilot was killed and the aircraft was left on site as its recovery was made impossible due to water constantly filling the excavation pit.

Date 11 July 1942
Aircraft F Battle Mk II L5717 1c OTU
Location Solway Firth
Reference 050540
Aircrew Kpl J Krzysztoszek p783216 PAF

After low flying over the sea near the weapons testing range, the aircraft plunged into the sea off Drumburgh, killing its crew and sinking.

Date 17 July 1942
Aircraft H Hurricane Mk I W9324 59 OTU 81 Grp
Location Aspatria
Reference 093420
Aircrew –

This pilot escaped unhurt after he made a crash-landing three miles west of Aspatria. The aircraft was removed by a salvage unit.

Date 18 July 1942
Aircraft H Hurricane Mk I V7008 55 OTU 81 Grp
Location Penrith
Reference 460311
Aircrew –

Engine failure caused the forced landing of this aircraft at Bunkers Hill. The pilot was unhurt and the aircraft removed by a salvage unit.

Date 20 July 1942
Aircraft H Hurricane Mk I R4217 59 OTU 81 Grp
Location Dowthwaite Head
Reference 370210
Aircrew –

This pilot escaped with minor injuries following a crash at Dowthwaite Head Farm. Most of the wreckage was removed but some fragments have been located.

Date 23 July 1942
Aircraft H Hurricane Mk I P2901 55 OTU
81 Grp
Location Lessonhall
Reference 229504
Aircrew –
Salvage units recovered this aircraft following an emergency landing near Lessonhall. The aircraft was on a training flight from RAF Annan.

Date 29 July 1942
Aircraft H Hurricane Mk I L1870 59 OTU
Location Aspatria
Reference 195424
Aircrew –
Another forced landing for this aircraft during a training flight from RAF Annan, this time at Watch Hill near Aspatria. The aircraft was removed by a salvage unit.

Date 1 August 1942
Aircraft M Master
Location Pooly Bridge
Reference 473246
Aircrew LR Disney
Flying from Lusworth to Ayre, an emergency landing was made in a corn field near Mains House Farm at Pooly Bridge. There were no injuries and the aircraft was removed by road. The aircraft's serial number was not recorded.

Date 10 August 1942
Aircraft H Hurricane (unidentified)
55 OTU
Location Kirkbride
Reference 230550
Aircrew –
Operating from RAF Annan, this aircraft made a forced landing on Kirkbride airfield following a mechanical failure. The aircraft was repaired on site and was returned into service a short time later.

Date 13 August 1942
Aircraft B Beaufort Mk II AW359
Location Silloth
Reference 126542
Aircrew F/O GB Critchley
Failure of the starboard engine during its take-off run was the cause of this crash-landing at the end of the runway. Crash teams recovered the aircraft.

Date 13 August 1942
Aircraft H Hurricane Mk I V7744 55 OTU
Location Penrith
Reference 456352
Aircrew –
A belly landing was made after this aircraft descended through low cloud over mountains. The pilot was uninjured and the aircraft recovered by road. The crash site was four miles north of Penrith at Unthank End.

Date 13 August 1942
Aircraft H Hurricane Mk I V7496
55 OTU
Location Kingstown
Reference 392594
Aircrew –
An engine failure during a training flight from RAF Annan caused the pilot to make a forced landing at Kingstown airfield. He was unhurt and the plane only slightly damaged.

Date 14 August 1942
Aircraft H Hurricane Mk I W7496
Location Kirkbride
Reference 230550
Aircrew –
An oil pressure failure forced the pilot of this aircraft to make an emergency landing on the airfield. Repairs to the aircraft were carried out on site and the aircraft returned to its base at RAF Annan two days later.

Date 14 August 1942
Aircraft H Hurricane Mk I V6857
55 OTU
Location Longtown
Reference 407715
Aircrew Sgt DRS Dixon NZ413822
Moments before this crash, the pilot was engaged in dog fighting practice at 4,000 feet; he then plunged to his death in Jean Syke Wood near Longtown.

It was thought that he had blacked out during a steep turn and was unconscious during the descent. The majority of the wreckage was removed by a salvage team.

Date	20 August 1942
Aircraft	H Hurricane Mk I Z4874
Location	Silloth
Reference	126542
Aircrew	–

After making a normal approach to land the pilot undershot the runway and landed with its undercarriage unlocked. The wheels folded up and the plane dropped on to its belly causing considerable damage. The cause was later traced to a faulty electrical selection switch.

Date	20 August 1942
Aircraft	V Wellington Mk Ic T2715
	25 OTU
Location	Millburn
Reference	762312
Aircrew	Sgt BG Crew

Shortly after eleven at night this aircraft crashed on the Water Shed at Greenburn in the Millburn Forest. The crew escaped from the aircraft though some were badly injured. The crash site is difficult to reach and salvage teams pushed the wreckage into rills on the fellside where it is today. Many parts can still be seen although they are not easy to find now and much is covered by soil.

Date	23 August 1942
Aircraft	H Hurricane Mk I Z7074
	55 OTU
Location	Kelsick
Reference	209508
Aircrew	Sgt Nice

While on a training flight from its base at RAF Annan this aircraft suffered an engine failure and made a forced landing in a field at Kelsick. The pilot was unhurt and the aircraft was removed by a salvage unit.

Date	24 August 1942
Aircraft	H Hurricane Mk I (unidentified)
Location	Wath Head (10 SLG)
Reference	–
Aircrew	–

On a training flight from its base at RAF Annan, a mechanical failure resulted in a forced landing at the satellite landing ground at Wath Head.

Date	25 August 1942
Aircraft	L Hudson Mk V AM676
	1c OTU
Location	Silloth
Reference	069460
Aircrew	Sgt RD McKenzie r85969 RCAF,
	Sgt EL Randell r92248 RCAF,
	F/Sgt McMillan r90126

Approximately half a mile to sea off Allonby lies the crash site of this Hudson lost during a training flight. Its crew were killed and the wreckage remains in the sands.

Date	26 August 1942
Aircraft	BL Botha Mk I L6245
Location	Cark
Reference	256572
Aircrew	–

The female ATA pilot of this Botha suffered an engine failure and was forced to make an emergency approach to RAF Cark. During the descent she had a near miss with another aircraft in the circuit and had to go around again. During the second circuit the remaining engine also failed and she crashed on the runway with the undercarriage retracted. She escaped with minor injuries and crash teams recovered the aircraft.

Date	27 August 1942
Aircraft	L Hudson Mk I N7226 1c OTU
Location	Millom
Reference	059458
Aircrew	–

A short distance off Dubmill Point is the crash site of this aircraft. Its crew were killed and although much of the wreckage was removed after the accident some parts of the aircraft can still be seen in the sands from time to time.

Date	31 August 1942
Aircraft	VS Spitfire Mk I N3265
Location	Millom
Reference	140790
Aircrew	–

During its finals to land, the flaps of this aircraft failed causing it to crash down onto the runway at

RAF Haverigg. The aircraft then swung off into soft ground and overturned; its pilot escaped unhurt.

Date	4 September 1942
Aircraft	V Wellington Mk Ic DV600
	25 OTU
Location	Keswick
Reference	248146
Aircrew	Sgt DE Derbyshire r102185,
	Sgt J Anderson 1292541,
	Sgt JL Brovendon r90611,
	Sgt WB Sage r105629,
	Sgt HB Burnett 952923

During a heavy thunderstorm at night, this aircraft was seen to drop flares in an attempt to verify its position. A short time later it crashed into a rock face above a wooded area on High Scawdell and exploded killing its crew. The accident happened while the aircraft was on a training flight from its base at RAF Finningley.

Wreckage was scattered over a wide area and a large burnt patch can still be seen on the rock face, other parts can be found in the woods although now covered with foliage.

Date	5 September 1942
Aircraft	H Hurricane Mk I Z4577
Location	Armthwaite
Reference	474485
Aircrew	Sgt LE Leavson

A forced landing near Moss Pool resulted from an engine failure during a training flight. The pilot was unhurt and the aircraft was recovered by a salvage team.

Date	6 September 1942
Aircraft	L Hudson Mk I N7725 1c OTU
Location	Cross Fell
Reference	686350
Aircrew	P/O PA Bourke 116160,
	Sgt LT Griffen 1380596,
	Sgt RA Hewett 1380777,
	Sgt R Band 1376686,
	Sgt J Bumpstead 1017138

Radio contact with this aircraft was lost at twelve thirty in the night, an extensive search was carried out at first light which located the

aircraft on Cross Fell, just below the summit. The aircraft had crashed there killing its crew. Some of the wreckage was removed while many other large sections were buried on site.

Date	7 September 1942
Aircraft	VS Spitfire (unidentified) 154 Sqd
Location	Kirkbride
Reference	230550
Aircrew	–

On a training flight from RAF Digby, the pilot made a forced landing at Kirkbride because of severe weather conditions. The weather improved and the aircraft was flown out a few days later.

Date	9 September 1942
Aircraft	VS Spitfire Mk Vb ER138 76MU
Location	Kirkbride
Reference	230550
Aircrew	1st Off IS Fossett ATA

Having left RAF Kinloss on the first leg of a delivery flight, the first uneventful stop was made at Prestwick. The second stop to collect maps for the next stage of the flight was at RAF Kirkbride. As the pilot approached the field he requested an emergency landing because of poor handling. An investigation following the landing found the aircraft's back to be broken and the airframe badly stressed, the cause traced to a bad take-off from Prestwick during which the tail of the aircraft was smashed down onto the runway during its take-off run.

Date	15 September 1942
Aircraft	G Wildcat Mk IV FN108
Location	Millom
Reference	230550
Aircrew	–

Damage to its number seven piston and cylinder was found to be the cause of this emergency landing at RAF Haverigg. The aircraft was repaired on site and returned into service.

Date	16 September 1942
Aircraft	H Hurricane Mk I (unidentified)
	55 OTU
Location	Wigton
Reference	265468
Aircrew	–

Airborne from RAF Annan on a training flight, a mechanical failure caused the pilot to force-land two miles south of Wigton. The pilot was unhurt and salvage teams later removed the aircraft by road.

Date 20 September 1942
Aircraft A Anson Mk II N4869
Location Muncaster Fell
Reference 140790
Aircrew Sgt C Kemp 650479, F/Sgt JW Jupp 909889 + 3 ANO

Very little now remains of this aircraft which crashed near the top of Muncaster Fell. Its crew were killed and the majority of the wreckage was removed or buried by a salvage unit.

Date 23 September 1942
Aircraft B Beaufighter Mk VI X8201 219 Sqd 13 Grp
Location Brayton Park
Reference 432194
Aircrew –

Flying from RAF Acklington with another aircraft, these aircraft were engaged on a practice interception exercise. Both aircraft had experienced difficulty with ground-to-air communications from their base. The pilot of this aircraft was heard to say that he was in trouble and was returning to base, in fact the aircraft crashed near the satellite landing ground at Brayton Park, Wigton. The impact caused a crater some thirty feet wide by fourteen feet deep and both crew members were killed. A crash investigation found some evidence showing that the pilot had tried to abandon his aircraft, but was unable to do so. The cause of the crash was listed as unknown; however, local residents say there was a very severe local storm in the area at the time of the crash.

Date 26 September 1942
Aircraft H Hurricane Mk XII JS303
Location Kirkbride
Reference 230550
Aircrew –

Flown by an ATA pilot this aircraft hit a petrol bowser on take-off, luckily there was no fire. The pilot was unhurt but the aircraft badly damaged.

Date 1 October 1942
Aircraft VS Spitfire AD235
Location Kirkbride
Reference 230550
Aircrew –

This aircraft made a forced landing on the airfield after its starboard wing failed under stress, caused by aerobatics.

Date 3 October 1942
Aircraft H Hurricane Mk IIc BN382 539 Sqd 13 Grp
Location Wylie Syke
Reference 661714
Aircrew F/Sgt BC Williams 405353

The soft boggy ground at Wylie Syke still holds the remains of this aircraft. It crashed in a steep dive killing its pilot. Rescue and salvage units were unable to recover the wreckage due to the wet ground and depth to which the aircraft had impacted into the ground. The aircraft was flying from RAF Acklington at the time of the crash.

Date 3 October 1942
Aircraft H Hurricane Mk I AG116
Location Silloth
Reference 126542
Aircrew ATA Station Officer PT Robinson

The pilot of this aircraft was badly injured after crashing onto the runway during take-off. The cause was an engine failure which left the pilot no time to lower his undercarriage.

Date 4 October 1942
Aircraft B Beaufighter Mk VI T5286 9 OTU 17 Grp
Location Crosby
Reference 432618
Aircrew F/O E Lyon 104429

Following a mechanical failure during a training flight, this aircraft crashed at Longpark killing its crew. The aircraft burned out and the wreckage was removed by crash teams.

Date 8 October 1942
Aircraft DH Tiger Moth Mk II T6559
15 EFTS
Location Rockcliff
Reference 330616
Aircrew P/O Berry 129227,
LAC SJ Ribbons 1397581
Both crew of this machine were killed after it crashed three miles west of Rockcliff. Crash teams removed the wreckage a short time later.

Date 14 October 1942
Aircraft Beechcraft AT8
Location Coniston
Reference 270982
Aircrew GW Branson + co-pilot
The cause of this accident is uncertain. The aircraft crashed into the summit of Coniston Old Man while on an ATA ferry flight. Its pilot was an employee of the Lockheed Aircraft Company. Although much of the wreckage was recovered by crash teams, some parts can still be seen above Low Water Tarn, other wreckage lies in the water.

Date 14 October 1942
Aircraft H Hurricane Mk I P3034 55 OTU
81 Grp
Location Carlisle
Reference 433591
Aircrew –
This training flight ended at White Close Gate when the pilot made an emergency landing. The aircraft was retrieved by a recovery team.

Date 30 October 1942
Aircraft M Master Mk I T8770
Location Penrith
Reference 494341
Aircrew Sgt MS Gilbert 1385416,
Sgt AM Wood 1337000
Low flying while beating up an Army convoy led to the aircraft hitting the ground at Kitchen Hill and disintegrating. Its crew were killed and the remains of the aircraft were removed by a crash team.

Date 10 November 1942
Aircraft L Hudson Mk V AM608
Location Martindale
Reference 429171
Aircrew P/O I Jones 120809, Sgt SA Veasy
12376462, Sgt JF Sanders
1266497, Sgt H Dickinson
1056292
A climb to Beda Head near Martindale will show the earthed-over wreckage of this aircraft where it crashed killing its crew. The majority of the remains are quite deep but some parts can be found near the surface.

Date 11 November 1942
Aircraft F Argus Mk I FK359
Location Kirkbride
Reference 230550
Aircrew –
While taxiing on the airfield, this aircraft ran into a second Argus. Both were damaged in the collision. They were later repaired on site and returned into service.

Date 12 November 1942
Aircraft V Wellington Mk III BK517
Location Millom
Reference 140790
Aircrew –
With one engine failure and the second engine's propeller beginning to break up, the pilot was prompted to make a forced landing at RAF Haverigg. The aircraft was repaired on site and later returned into service.

Date 13 November 1942
Aircraft VS Seafire Mk IIc MB238
Location Kirkbride
Reference 230550
Aircrew F/O RA Gibson
An ATA pilot made a landing with his flaps fully up due to a mechanical failure. With 400 yards of airfield left he managed to land but then overshot the runway and turned over in soft ground. The pilot was unhurt, but the aircraft was badly damaged. It was removed by a crash team.

Date 13 November 1942
Aircraft L Hudson Mk I N7207
Location Silloth
Reference 172565
Aircrew Sgt J Fisher 1218315,
Sgt R Creighton 1029162 2 ANOs
Apart from police and station records noting this aircraft crashing and killing its crew of four in Morecambe Bay, no other information is available.

Date 14 November 1942
Aircraft G Wildcat Mk IV FN243
Location Kirkbride
Reference 230550
Aircrew –
The pilot of this aircraft forgot to lock the tail wheel during take-off which resulted in the tail swinging off the runway causing the main under-carriage to collapse. The aircraft was badly damaged as it crashed onto its underside. It was later repaired on site and returned into service.

Date 14 November 1942
Aircraft L Hudson Ic OTU
Location Kirkbride
Reference 230550
Aircrew –
After swinging off the runway during take-off, this aircraft crashed into a parked Spitfire. Both aircraft were damaged but fortunately the crew were unhurt.

Date 15 November 1942
Aircraft P Proctor Mk III HM353
Location Kirkbride
Reference 230550
Aircrew –
During its take-off run, this aircraft rolled over nose first. Though extensively damaged its pilot was unhurt, and a later investigation found a fault in the braking system which caused the wheels to lock.

Date 18 November 1942
Aircraft HP Hampden Mk I TB P1356
Location Millom
Reference 140790
Aircrew –
A loss of oil pressure resulted in a complete

engine failure. The pilot made an emergency landing at RAF Haverigg. The aircraft was repaired on site and later returned to service.

Date 20 November 1942
Aircraft VS Spitfire Mk Vb AD544 222 Sqd
Location Martindale
Reference 456204
Aircrew F/O RS Strozak e1789 PAF
Wreckage from this aircraft can still be located on Swarthbeck Fell above Martindale. Flying from Ayr it crashed killing its pilot.

Date 22 November 1942
Aircraft S Stirling Mk I BF404
Location Kirkbride
Reference 230550
Aircrew –
A failure of the starboard inboard engine resulted in a circuit of the airfield followed by an emergency landing. There was little damage and the aircraft returned into service following repairs.

Date 30 November 1942
Aircraft L Hudson Mk I N7207
Location Silloth
Reference 164564
Aircrew Sgt Brunton, Sgt Crighton,
Sgt Fisher, Sgt Brack
The crew of this aircraft were killed as it crashed into Morecambe Bay. Wreckage from the aircraft was left on site although it is now buried in the sands.

Date 6 December 1942
Aircraft H Hurricane Mk I R4230
Location Carlisle
Reference 452508
Aircrew Sgt CRF Shackell 1315125
A Canadian pilot serving in the RAF was killed when his aircraft crashed near Cocklakes Plaster Works. The wreckage of the aircraft was removed by a salvage team a few days later.

Date 14 December 1942
Aircraft A Oxford Mk I HN428
Location Silloth
Reference 126542
Aircrew ATA Station Officer H Thomas
Flown by an ATA pilot, this aircraft struck a tree

while approaching the airfield. Although a propeller was damaged, the pilot managed to land the aircraft without further mishap. The aircraft was repaired on site and later returned into service.

Date	15 December 1942
Aircraft	H Hector K9760
Location	Millom
Reference	140790
Aircrew	–

Following an engine failure on take-off, this aircraft crash-landed in a small field near the runway. The aircraft was recovered by a crash team.

Date	16 December 1942
Aircraft	V Wellington Mk III X3336 23 OTU
Location	Careside Fell, Skiddaw
Reference	250285
Aircrew	TS Bellew 655304, RV Walker j13418, P/O A Higgins 1317232, AS Dubben 1381897, GW Hicks 124319, P/O RS Goodwin R Lawton

Flying from its base at RAF Pershore, this aircraft crashed into Ullock Pike in poor weather conditions and exploded killing its crew. Wreckage was scattered over a wide area and down the fell side, and many fragments of the aircraft can still be found on the slopes below the point of impact.

Date	17 December 1942
Aircraft	H Hurricane Mk I AG282 55 OTU
Location	Kirkbrampton
Reference	262564
Aircrew	Sgt K Holden 1025981

Station records show this aircraft as crashing near Studholme killing its pilot. No other information was recorded.

Date	21 December 1942
Aircraft	D Boston Mk III W8273
Location	Kirkbride
Reference	230550
Aircrew	F/O CW Totto

Following a normal landing, the nose wheel of this aircraft collapsed and it crashed down onto

the runway travelling some considerable distance before coming to a halt. Its crew were unhurt and an investigation later proved a fault in the hydraulic system.

Date	21 December 1942
Aircraft	F Battle Mk I T P6638
Location	Cark
Reference	256572
Aircrew	–

The pilot of this aircraft received a commendation for his skill in landing this aircraft which was badly damaged. The accident occurred when the aircraft became enmeshed with the steel cable of a target towing aircraft which had flown across the Battle's path.

Date	27 December 1942
Aircraft	W Lysander Mk III T1674
Location	Low Scales
Reference	169818
Aircrew	–

During a training flight from its base at RAF Wallney Island, a mechanical failure forced the crew to make a crash-landing at Low Scales near Millom. The crew were unhurt and the aircraft was removed by a salvage team.

Date	27 December 1942
Aircraft	Unidentified
Location	Millom Bay
Reference	Uncertain
Aircrew	–

Police reports describe an aircraft being seen to crash into Millom Bay and sink. No further details are known.

Date	28 December 1942
Aircraft	H Hurricane Mk I W9233 55 OTU H Hurricane Mk I AG150
Location	Longtown
Reference	420724 428728
Aircrew	Sgt AV Marshall 1332781, Sgt GH Walsh 657583

Following a mid-air collision, both aircraft crashed near Lamb Hill Farm, at Brisco Hill. With virtually no time to escape from their aircraft, both pilots were killed. The wreckage was removed by a salvage team.

Date 1 January 1943
Aircraft A Anson Mk I AX145 1(c) AFU
A Anson Mk I W2629 1(c) AFU
Location Skiddaw
Reference 318352 / 306354
Aircrew Sgt WBC Thompson j16171,
Sgt EO Knight 414374, P/O W
Burt 129765, BO Brown 129765,
Sgt WFL Babbington NZ39816

These aircraft were engaged on a night flying exercise from their base at Wigtown. They were reported as missing after they became overdue. Meanwhile workers at the barytes mines heard an aircraft pass low overhead in thick cloud followed by a loud crash. As they made their way up the fell side to investigate, they came across one of the aircrew who was staggering down to find help. The workers recovered the body of one crew member who was killed in the impact and rescued another. A short time later and only a few miles away, the second aircraft crashed near Hay Gill, killing its crew. However this aircraft was not found until nearly one month later. Salvage units recovered the wreckage of both aircraft with the use of horses and sledges because of the weather conditions and inaccessibility of the crash site. Only a few fragments of the aircraft at Hay Gill can be seen today.

Date 4 January 1943
Aircraft L Hudson Mk I N7308
Location Solway Firth
Reference 146573
Aircrew Pilot DJ Wearne Aus408544
Nav LF Ryan Aus416368

While making an approach to RAF Silloth, this aircraft crashed into the sea off Grune Point killing its crew. Little was recovered from the site and much of the wreckage remains in the sand.

Date 9 January 1943
Aircraft A Lancaster Mk 1 ED394 50 Sqd
Location Brampton
Reference 510607
Aircrew W/O G Sunley 159008, Sgt AS
Langly 1514232, Sgt HJ Huxman
1585578, Sgt T Harrower 617248,
Sgt Smith

Few Lancaster bombers were lost in the Lake District. In this accident a crew of five were killed after their aircraft crashed returning from a raid on Germany. After crossing the coast the aircraft was diverted to RAF Crosby to avoid bad weather near its home base. Landing at night the aircraft bounced on the runway, and the pilot decided to make another circuit. On its second approach the aircraft hit the ground in a field near Hollingstones, crashing across a road and through a hedge, the aircraft finally came to rest against a farmhouse breaking up as it skidded along the ground. Fuel from the aircraft's tanks was sprayed over farm buildings which then ignited. The resulting fire killed and injured a number of dogs in kennels at the farm, and also caused ammunition to explode in the flames.

Date 9 January 1943
Aircraft VS Spitfire Mk Vc JG953
Location Kirkbride
Reference 230550
Aircrew –

A lady ATA pilot overshot the runway while landing, overturning the aircraft in soft ground. She escaped unhurt and the aircraft was returned into service following repairs.

Date 10 January 1943
Aircraft B Beaufighter Mk Ic T5103
9 OTU
Location Crosby
Reference 480605
Aircrew –

Following a normal landing the undercarriage of this aircraft collapsed. The crew were unhurt and the plane returned into service following repairs. The aircraft was lost in an accident in April 1944.

Date 13 January 1943
Aircraft L Hudson Mk I T9322 1c OTU
Location Silloth
Reference 120542
Aircrew Sgt C Ring 1384726,
Sgt JW Sawerson 942817,
Sgt FC Zurbrigg r11656 RCAF,
W/O JLG Belanger r73758

This aircraft crashed on the airfield and burned out. Its crew were killed in the impact. The wreckage was removed by a crash team.

Date 13 January 1943
Aircraft DH Tiger Moth Mk II T6499
DH Tiger Moth Mk I BB755
(G-ADXE)
Location Burnfoot
Reference 1262542
Aircrew –

One aircraft trying to take-off, another trying to land at the same time was the recipe for this accident on Burnfoot airfield. Both aircraft crashed on the airfield, with two airmen being badly injured and the other two only slightly injured.

Date 20 January 1943
Aircraft B Skua
Location Haverigg
Reference 140790
Aircrew W Mougeridge

Records show that this aircraft crash-landed at RAF Haverigg due to a mechanical failure, and that the aircraft was submerged by the incoming tide. Its recovery took place some time later. This suggests that the accident was on the foreshore at Haverigg.

Date 20 January 1943
Aircraft H Henley L3408
Location Methop
Reference 457812
Aircrew ATA Second Officer RH Badhe

Local people saw this aircraft flying low over Methop village with black smoke coming from its engine. Villagers said that it looked as if the pilot was trying to find somewhere to land. The aircraft finally crashed into a small wood after its wing hit a tree where it burned out killing its pilot. The crater caused by the impact can still be seen together with a few fragments of the aircraft scattered around. An investigation found that the accident had been caused by water in the aircraft's carburettors.

Date 21 January 1943
Aircraft VS Spitfire Mk IIa P7889
Location Kirkbride
Reference 230550
Aircrew –

While this aircraft was taxying on the airfield piloted by a female ATA pilot, observers reported excessive use of the brakes. Eventually, the brakes jammed on and the aircraft turned over nose first. The pilot was unhurt and the aircraft was repaired in situ and returned into service some time later.

Date 21 January 1943
Aircraft H Hurricane Mk I AF959 55 OTU
Location Skiddaw
Reference 262309
Aircrew Sgt DL Baker 656680

This aircraft flew into flat ground at Nelliess End on Skiddaw. It overturned killing its pilot and was completely destroyed. The aircraft was reported as overdue and an extensive search was carried out. The plane was eventually located some six days after the crash. Some remains can still be seen at the site. Records show that this aircraft may have crashed some six months prior to being found.

Date 27 January 1943
Aircraft B Beaufort Mk II DD880
Location Longtown
Reference 405686
Aircrew Sgt LF Simpson 1319895, Sgt J
Jones 1101023

The pilot and his observer were both killed as the aircraft crashed near Hallburn. The wreckage was removed by a salvage team.

Date 29 January 1943
Aircraft B Botha Mk I L6184
Location Silloth
Reference 126542
Aircrew –

An investigation failed to find the cause of this aircraft's undercarriage collapsing following a normal landing. The ATA delivery crew were unhurt and repairs were carried out on site. The aircraft was returned into service.

Date 3 February 1943
Aircraft VS Spitfire Mk I X4411
Location Kirkbride
Reference 230550
Aircrew –

This Spitfire was destroyed after a Hudson bomber suffered an engine failure during take-off and crashed on top of it. Details of the Hudson were not recorded.

Date 8 February 1943
Aircraft A Anson Mk I AX293
Location Millom
Reference 124311
Aircrew F/Sgt H Smith 641453, Sgt A Page 1312911, Sgt TJ Thompson 515446, Sgt JG Hardie
After crashing in shallow water off Haverigg this aircraft sank killing its crew. Salvage teams removed the wreckage a short time later.

Date 10 February 1943
Aircraft DH Tiger Moth Mk II T5955
15 EFTS
Location Solway Firth
Reference 150590
Aircrew –
Mechanical failure caused the pilot to ditch his plane in the sea. He escaped unhurt as the aircraft sank.

Date 13 February 1943
Aircraft unknown
Location Weatheral
Reference Unknown
Aircrew –
Apart from a very sparse police report of this accident, no other information is available.

Date 14 February 1943
Aircraft BP Defiant Mk II N1551
Location North of Barrow
Reference 265830
Aircrew Station Officer RW Reisent
An ATA pilot lost control of his aircraft in poor weather conditions. After spinning twice and recovering, he baled out of the plane. It crashed a short distance away and the wreckage was recovered by a salvage unit.

Date 15 February 1943
Aircraft A Anson Mk II DJ464
Location Hobcarton End
Reference 198239
Aircrew F/Sgt AJ Jeague 1280780,
Sgt WM Carlvey 1333062,
LAC H Buckly 859037,
LAC AE Austin 1601636

A climb to this location will still show a few remains of this aircraft which crashed during a training flight from its base. Its crew were killed and most of the wreckage was removed by a salvage unit.

Date 16 February 1943
Aircraft A Anson
Location Cross Fell
Reference 692344
Aircrew 1st Off MA Murtagh
While an ATA pilot was delivering this aircraft, en route from RAF Kinloss to RAF Kirkbride he encountered poor weather near Penrith. He was forced to fly south down the Alston valley and flew into flat ground on Cross Fell. A search for the aircraft was started and the pilot was found by two police officers, inside the aircraft wrapped in his parachute suffering from a broken leg and severe facial injuries. He was taken to hospital for treatment. When salvage teams reached the aircraft they found that most of the items of value had been stolen. The wreckage was removed and some buried on site on 3 March. Many of the crashed aircraft and their crew were looted by visitors to the crash sites often before they were reported, something which still happens today.

Date 17 February 1943
Aircraft DH Tiger Moth Mk II T1712
15 EFTS
Location Binsey Hill
Reference 225355
Aircrew F/O AE Woodley 109066
A flying instructor was killed when his aircraft crashed at Binsey Hill, north of Keswick. The wreckage was removed by salvage teams.

Date 24 February 1943
Aircraft V Wellington Mk X MF571
Location Millom
Reference 140790
Aircrew –
Following a normal landing at RAF Haverigg, a fault in the braking system caused the aircraft to turn over nose first. Repairs were carried out on site and the aircraft returned to service some time later.

The following sequence of photographs formed part of the accident
inquiry into the Lancaster crash at
Hollingstones. (Crown copyright)

(1) Close up of the impact point.
(Crown copyright)

(2) Impact point two.
(Crown copyright)

(3) Point three, closing on the house. (Crown copyright)

(4) Point four, the aircraft passed over the roadway. (Crown copyright)

(5) Wreckage from the aircraft scattered across the field. (Crown copyright)

(6) Part of the wing against the garden wall.
(Crown copyright)

(7) Point of impact with the house and the seat of the fire.
(Crown copyright)

(8) The burnt out wreckage and dog kennels.
(Crown copyright)

Date 26 February 1943
Aircraft H Hurricane Mk I P8813
55 OTU
Location Bewcastle Fell
Reference 562817
Aircrew Sgt RV Kennady r136199
On a cross-country training flight from its base at RAF Annan, this aircraft crashed at Bewcastle killing its pilot. Most of the wreckage was removed but some parts can still be located.

Date 28 February 1943
Aircraft H Hurricane Mk I V6573
H Hurricane Mk I W9170
Location Blackford
Reference 633625 / 633629
Aircrew Sgt RD Fatig r126851
After a mid-air collision one aircraft crashed near Blackford killing its pilot. The pilot of the second managed to escape and landed about a mile away. The wreckage of both aircraft was removed by salvage units.

Date 2 March 1943
Aircraft DH Tiger Moth Mk II N9462
15 EFTS
Location Solway Firth
Reference 167609
Aircrew –
The crew of this plane escaped after they ditched into the Solway Firth. The plane sank and was not recovered.

Date 3 March 1943
Aircraft DH Tiger Moth Mk II T8033
15 EFTS
Location Kingstown
Reference 392594
Aircrew –
The crew of this aircraft scrambled unhurt from the wreckage after they taxied into soft ground and overturned on the airfield.

Date 8 March 1943
Aircraft P Proctor Mk III HM367
Location Kirkbride
Reference 230550
Aircrew –
Following a normal landing this aircraft was hit

by a strong tail wind which turned the aircraft over. Although the plane was badly damaged its pilot was unhurt.

Date 9 March 1943
Aircraft B Beaufighter Mk VIc T5158
(369)
Location Brampton
Reference 519618
Aircrew F/O RD Jones RAFVR 126150,
Sgt JP Longlands 947052,
Sgt BW Tully NZ416558
During a training flight from RAF Crosby this aircraft crashed close to the airfield killing its crew. The wreckage was removed by a salvage unit.

Date 12 March 1943
Aircraft V Wellington Mk X HX713
Location Millom
Reference 140790
Aircrew –
An ATA pilot received a commendation for his skill in landing this aircraft after a mechanical failure caused one of its engines to feather, and the second engine to run rough. The aircraft was repaired on site and later returned into service.

Date 12 March 1943
Aircraft A Lancaster Mk I ED614
Location Kirkbride
Reference 230550
Aircrew –
A coolant failure followed by an engine failure caused the pilot to make a forced landing on the airfield. Repairs were carried out and the aircraft returned into service a short time later.

Date 3 April 1943
Aircraft V Walrus Mk I X9482
Location Kirkbride
Reference 230550
Aircrew –
The pilot of this aircraft lost control after being caught by a strong crosswind while landing. The aircraft ground looped, crashed onto the runway and was extensively damaged.

Date 8 April 1943
Aircraft VS Spitfire Mk Vc JL224
Location Kirkbride
Reference 230550
Aircrew –
Following an engine failure during take-off, the aircraft overshot the runway and turned on to its nose. Repairs were carried out on site and the aircraft later returned into service.

Date 8 April 1943
Aircraft A Anson Mk I M652 EG361
Location Keswick
Reference 207265
Aircrew P/O RA Duff j21885,
P/O MH Finbow j14741,
Sgt H Mosgy 657927,
Sgt Gooney 974034,
B Robertson Marshall
After this aircraft was reported overdue a full-scale search was started. The aircraft was located by the pilot of a Lysander flying over Lord's Seat near Keswick the Anson had crashed in poor weather killing all but one of its crew. Unfortunately the surviving crew member died shortly after rescue teams reached the crash site. The majority of the wreckage was removed, although some parts have been found at the crash site.

Date 11 April 1943
Aircraft H Hurricane Mk I v6884
Location Wigton
Reference 155510
Aircrew F/O CA Fawcett 80248
The pilot was killed and his aircraft destroyed after crashing into Kingside Hill. The wreckage was removed by a salvage team.

Date 11 April 1943
Aircraft H Hurricane Mk I V6887 22 OTU
Location Silloth
Reference 157464
Aircrew F/O Howett
This Hurricane crashed the same day four miles south-east of Silloth airfield at Lancrigg. Its pilot was killed and the plane burned out. The wreckage was later removed by a salvage team.

Date 12 April 1943
Aircraft DH Tiger Moth Mk I T5143
Location Carlisle
Reference 415576
Aircrew –
After flying into low cloud during a training flight, the crew of this aircraft became lost and made a forced landing near Carlisle. The crew were unhurt and the aircraft recovered by a crash team a short time later.

Date 15 April 1943
Aircraft B Beaufighter Mk VI JL566
9 OTU 17 Grp
Location Cardurnock
Reference 171592
Aircrew –
An aircraft from 'C Squadron' crashed near the village killing its crew. The wreckage was removed by a crash team a few days later.

Date 15 April 1943
Aircraft H Hurricane Mk I AF984
55 OTU
Location Nicol Forest
Reference 485795
Aircrew W/O WM Hicks r91878
Another pilot lost his life when his plane crashed at Robbens Glen. Much of the wreckage was removed though some parts have been found at the site.

Date 23 April 1943
Aircraft H Hurricane Mk I AG264
55 OTU
H Hurricane Mk I AG275
20 AFU 2(o)AFU
Location Coniston
Reference 276988 / 273991
Aircrew Sgt HM Atherton Aus414123,
Sgt LT Cook Aus412399
Wreckage from these aircraft can be found above Coniston. Both crashed following a mid-air collision on a Good Friday. One hit Brimm Fell and exploded killing its pilot and scattering wreckage over a wide area. The second aircraft hit Raven Tor and also exploded killing its pilot. The wreckage is scattered down the fell side and some lies in small streams.

Date 24 April 1943
Aircraft V Wellington Mk X HE496 6
(c) OTU
Location Solway Firth
Reference 930270
Aircrew F/O FK Dostal 131537

After smoke was seen rising from the sea off Silloth, an air-sea rescue operation was put into action. It transpired that this aircraft had crashed in flames killing its crew but no bodies were recovered. Two months later the body of one crew member was recovered from the water. The wreckage of the aircraft remains in the sea.

Date 27 April 1943
Aircraft AW Whitley Mk V BD263
19 OTU
Location Silloth
Reference 126542
Aircrew –

On loan to Silloth from its base at RAF Kinloss, the aircraft overshot the runway while landing and crashed into two petrol bowsers. The bowsers burst into flames as the crew leapt from the aircraft uninjured.

Date 28 April 1943
Aircraft H Hurricane Mk I P3901
Location Croglin
Reference 600475
Aircrew F/Sgt P Skoblack r59063 RCAF

This pilot flying from RAF Annan was killed after he crashed his aircraft into Scarrow Fell above Croglin. Most of the remains were removed although some parts can be found at the site.

Date 4 May 1943
Aircraft DH Tiger Moth Mk I N9367
Location Kingstown
Reference 230550
Aircrew –

This aircraft crashed on the airfield during a night flying exercise. Its crew were slightly injured but the aircraft was badly damaged.

Wreckage from Hurricane AG275 on Brimm Fell. The pistons and wing sections can be clearly seen.
(J Huggon)

Date　　　7 May 1943
Aircraft　　V Wellington
Location　　Silloth
Reference　126542
Aircrew　　−

A report in station records logs a Wellington as crashing on the airfield during a flight check. Its crew were unhurt but the plane was badly damaged. The identity of the aircraft was not recorded.

Date　　　15 May 1943
Aircraft　　H Hurricane
Location　　Ireby
Reference　244387
Aircrew　　−

Very few details are recorded regarding this accident other than the pilot being unhurt following a crash near Ireby.

Date　　　19 May 1943
Aircraft　　H Hurricane Mk II Z2978
Location　　Westlinton
Reference　347640
Aircrew　　P/O JLA Wellenkens 141836

Salvage units removed the wreckage from this aircraft after it crashed near Blackford, Westlinton killing its pilot. No other details were recorded.

Date　　　20 May 1943
Aircraft　　M Magister Mk I T9835
Location　　Barrow in Furness
Reference　142751
Aircrew　　Cadet KG Caserson (Danish ATA)

An engine failure caused the Danish ATA pilot to ditch his aircraft in the sea between Barrow and Millom. At the time of the crash the pilot was in breach of regulations, low flying over water. After the ditching the aircraft stayed afloat for some time and sank while being towed ashore by a rescue boat. The pilot was unhurt.

Date　　　25 May 1943
Aircraft　　B Beaufighter Mk Ic T4763
　　　　　　　9 OTU
Location　　Brampton
Reference　528625
Aircrew　　Sgt D Mason 1332898,
　　　　　　　Sgt P Allport 1247249

The pilot and his navigator were killed after the aircraft crashed at Brecon Hill near Brampton. The wreckage was removed by a salvage unit.

Date　　　27 May 1943
Aircraft　　H Hurricane Mk I P3039
　　　　　　　55 OTU
Location　　Silloth
Reference　093455
Aircrew　　F/O MS McQualter Aus413014

Crash teams recovered the body of the pilot following this accident at Edderside. The wreckage was removed later.

Date　　　27 May 1943
Aircraft　　A Anson (C6) (C Sqd)
Location　　Silloth
Reference　126542
Aircrew　　−

As it approached number three runway this aircraft stalled and crashed onto the airfield. Although badly damaged the crew escaped unhurt. The station's log reports this accident but the aircraft's identity is uncertain as it was identified only by its call sign of C6.

Date　　　28 May 1943
Aircraft　　A Anson Mk I AX407
Location　　Millom
Reference　109800
Aircrew　　Sgt SP James 1338360

This aircraft sank with its crew after it crashed into the sea off Silecroft. The wreckage of the aircraft is still in the sands.

Date　　　31 May 1943
Aircraft　　L Hudson Mk III V9197
Location　　Kirkbride
Reference　230550
Aircrew　　F/O P Freugh

This crew had a lucky escape after their aircraft was hit by a strong crosswind during take-off. It was lifted into the air where it stalled and cartwheeled onto the runway. The plane was extensively damaged and removed by a salvage team.

Date	31 May 1943
Aircraft	A Anson Mk I DJ239 (10)
	(0) AFU
	V Wellington Mk VIII HZ637
	41 Grp
Location	Maryport
Reference	044365
Aircrew	P/O AI McRae 16366,
	JT Sutherland 421474,
	Sgt GBT Wymer 1382991,
	T Green 1027817,
	F/Lt WJ Calver 44751 1 ANO

Six aircrew died following a mid-air collision. The aircraft crashed close to the Ellonbrough Road and the nearby railway lines. The wreckage of both aircraft was removed by crash teams.

Date	16 June 1943
Aircraft	V Wellington Mk Ic HE982
	H Hurricane Mk IIc LB612 22 MU
Location	Silloth
Reference	126542
Aircrew	–

An instructor pilot overshot the number three runway while landing at RAF Silloth. The aircraft then crashed into a parked Hurricane. The pilot was unhurt but both aircraft were badly damaged.

Date	17 June 1943
Aircraft	B Beaufighter Mk XI JM129
	9 OTU
Location	Silloth
Reference	126542
Aircrew	–

During a training flight from its base at RAF Crosby, this aircraft crashed near Silloth airfield. The wreckage was removed by a salvage team.

Date	23 June 1943
Aircraft	H Hurricane Mk IIb BE489
	H Hurricane Mk IIb Z2687
Location	Cumwhinton
Reference	448520 / 455525
Aircrew	Sgt PM Clark Aus12903,
	WD Graves j10285

Another mid-air collision which killed both pilots. The first aircraft crashed near Brockelwath Farm, the second came down close to the river. The wreckage of both aircraft was removed by crash teams.

Date	28 June 1943
Aircraft	V Wellington Mk Ic HE258 6
	(c) OTU
Location	Silloth
Reference	095518
Aircrew	F/O DG Mann NZ401211

The navigator of this aircraft was drowned after it crashed off West Beach Silloth; the remaining crew were rescued. At the time of the accident the aircraft was taking part in a training exercise. Salvage teams removed the wreckage over a number of days between tides.

Date	4 July 1943
Aircraft	B Beaufighter Mk XI JM223
	1c OTU
Location	Croglin Fell
Reference	60448800
Aircrew	P/O HJ Carver J14852,
	F/O RA Sedgley 135618

Four miles north-east of Croglin on the fell side is the crash site of this aircraft where it exploded killing its crew. The fell still bears the mark of the intense fire. The majority of the wreckage was removed by crash teams, though some still lies buried on site.

Date	8 July 1943
Aircraft	H Hurricane Mk V (NL)
	55 OTU
Location	Aspatria
Reference	135419
Aircrew	–

An engine failure caused this aircraft to make a forced landing in a field near Broughton Hall. The pilot was unhurt and the aircraft was recovered later by a salvage unit.

Date	11 July 1943
Aircraft	B Beaufighter Mk VIc X8036
	9 OTU
Location	Wigton
Reference	194432
Aircrew	Sgt AM Vinton 658359,
	Sgt HJ Shallow 1414529

The navigator of this aircraft was killed in the

impact as the aircraft crashed a few miles from Wigton. The pilot was released from the wreckage by a rescue team but died later in hospital. The wreckage was removed by a salvage unit.

Date 13 July 1943
Aircraft B Beaufort Mk I JM589
Location Kirkbride
Reference 230550
Aircrew –
Flown by an ATA pilot, the aircraft hit a truck while taking off. It was damaged but after a number of circuits the pilot decided to continue with his flight rather than land on the airfield. On reaching his destination, the aircraft crashed.

Date 16 July 1943
Aircraft B Beaufighter Mk Ic T3352
9 OTU
Location Cumwhinton
Reference 449530
Aircrew –
This aircraft crashed and burned out near Stockdale Hall. Fortunately, with the exception of one minor injury, none of the crew was hurt. The wreckage was removed by a salvage team.

Date 16 July 1943
Aircraft B Beaufighter Mk Vc T5335
Location Irthington
Reference 493605
Aircrew Sgt J Beanland 1148602,
Sgt GLF Philcox 1399431
The crew of this aircraft were killed after it crashed at Beanlands, near Irthington. The wreckage was removed by a salvage unit.

Date 18 July 1943
Aircraft A Lancaster Mk I W4947
1661 HCU
Location Millom
Reference 110790
Aircrew Sgt CG Hirst 1320056,
Sgt GD Leverton 1577248,
P/O C Dykes 137546,
Sgt TH Loftus 1600812
Half a mile out to sea off Silecroft is the resting place of this bomber from RAF Winthorpe. It crashed with the loss of its crew. Little was

recovered from the aircraft and the bodies of its crew were washed ashore several months later.

Date 21 July 1943
Aircraft A Anson (S-SMI)
Location Kirkbride
Reference 115820
Aircrew –
This aircraft crashed into the sea off Silecroft and its crew were rescued by an air-sea rescue launch. The aircraft sank and many parts remain in the sands. The records of this accident log the aircraft only by its code letters.

Date 23 July 1943
Aircraft V Wellington Mk X HE305
Location RAF Silloth
Reference 126542
Aircrew Sgt WT McKenzie 1525454
A brief account of this accident appears in station records; it crashed on the airfield with loss of life. No other details were recorded.

Date 23 July 1943
Aircraft DH Tiger Moth Mk II T6498
Location Westlinton
Reference 395622
Aircrew F/Sgt HD Bryson 134405
Another brief account of an accident appears in station records. This aircraft crashed at Westlinton with loss of life. No other details were recorded.

Date 24 July 1943
Aircraft P Proctor Mk III Z7214
VS Spitfire
Location Kirkbride
Reference 230550
Aircrew –
This aircraft swung off the runway while landing and crashed into a parked Spitfire. An investigation traced the cause to a malfunction in the braking system. The identity of the Spitfire was not recorded.

Date 3 August 1943
Aircraft V Wellington (No 5)
Location Silloth
Reference 126542
Aircrew –

An account in station records shows that this aircraft's undercarriage collapsed as it landed on the airfield. It was later repaired on site and returned into service. No accurate record was made of its serial number, it being recorded by its code number.

Date	4 August 1943
Aircraft	B Beaufighter Mk I L9963
	9 OTU
Location	Longtown
Reference	410680
Aircrew	–

The tail of this aircraft was chopped off by the propeller of another aircraft after collision on the taxi track at RAF Longtown. The accident occurred at the start of a night training exercise.

Date	4 August 1943
Aircraft	B Beaufort Mk I L9819
	9 (c) OTU
Location	Longtown
Reference	383672
Aircrew	P/O HG Miller J21964
	W/O RJ Badger 1376786

Later the same evening this Beaufort, also engaged on the night flying exercise, was reported overdue. The following morning the aircraft was found alongside the Longtown to Carlisle road with its crew dead inside. The wreckage was removed by a salvage unit.

Date	9 August 1943
Aircraft	A Anson Mk I M5053 10 (o) AFU
	29 Grp
Location	Great Dodd
Reference	344205
Aircrew	W MacKenzie 79491

The ninth of August was a bad evening for flying accidents when four Ansons from the same unit crashed in the Lakes. The aircraft were all taking part in a cross-country night flying exercise from RAF Brampton. Incorrect meteorological reports were noted as a contributing factor in these accidents, after the aircraft drifted into the mountains. One member of the crew was killed in this crash. This aircraft crashed on Great Dodd near Keswick. Wreckage can still be found at its crash

site although the remains can be difficult to locate now.

Date	9 August 1943
Aircraft	A Anson Mk I LS986 4 AFU
	29 Grp
Location	Heskit
Reference	344348
Aircrew	–

The crew of this aircraft escaped unhurt after it crash-landed near Carrock Beck, Heskit. The badly damaged aircraft was removed by a salvage unit.

Date	9 August 1943
Aircraft	A Anson Mk I DJ275 10 (c) AFU
	29 Grp
Location	Scafell
Reference	212058
Aircrew	W Mackiewicz 79491 PAF
	+ 4 ANO

The crew of this aircraft died when it crashed and exploded on Cam Spout Cragg. Wreckage from the plane can still be found near and below the crash site.

Date	9 August 1943
Aircraft	A Anson Mk I DJ222 10 (o) AFU
	29 Grp
Location	Green Gable
Reference	205218
Aircrew	F/Sgt EA Loppe r176010 RCAF,
	Sgt D Ppausil 794954 PAF
	LAC, JA Price 1017530

Two crew of this aircraft died after it flew into flat ground at Green Gable. A climb to the crash site will reveal some wreckage from the aircraft.

Date	19 August 1943
Aircraft	G Hellcat Mk I FN355
Location	Millom
Reference	140790
Aircrew	–

Following an engine failure on take-off the pilot made a crash-landing on the airfield at RAF Haverigg. The undercarriage was up and the aircraft was badly damaged, its pilot escaped without injury.

Wreckage from Anson M5053 on Great Dodd. (MJ Hurst)

Date 20 August 1943
Aircraft V Wellington Mk Ic X3986 6 Sqd 1 (c) OTU
Location Silloth
Reference 093523
Aircrew Sgt FJ Manley 1452197,
Sgt J Waugh 1484114,
Sgt HL Griffiths 1367513,
Sgt GM Jackson 1394331

A strong gale and high seas prevented three air-sea rescue launches from sailing to try and locate a Wellington bomber which had crashed in the Solway Firth off West Beach. The aircraft was not recovered and its crew were killed in the accident. The body of one crew member was washed into Silloth Dock a week later, and the bodies of the remaining crew were recovered in mid-September.

Date 22 August 1943
Aircraft B Beaufighter Mk Ic T4721 9 OTU
Location Warwick Bridge
Reference 495575
Aircrew Sgt K Pumphrey 1503509

The crew of this aircraft were freed from the wreckage by locals after it crashed near Corry

House, Topping Castle during a training flight from RAF Crosby. The crew were taken to hospital at Carlisle where the pilot died of his injuries. The wreckage was later removed by a salvage unit.

Date 24 August 1943
Aircraft B Beaufighter Mk VI EL362 9 OTU
Location Scaleby
Reference 456634
Aircrew –

This aircraft crashed five miles from its base killing the pilot. The wreckage was removed by a salvage team.

Date 26 August 1943
Aircraft H Hurricane Mk V KZ579
Location Kirkbride
Reference 230550
Aircrew –

During an ATA delivery flight this pilot crashed into a parked lorry while landing, he was only slightly injured. The same, however, could not be said of the aircraft which was badly damaged.

Date 27 August 1943
Aircraft B Beaufort
Location Solway Firth
Reference 230550
Aircrew –
Operating from its base at RAF Longtown, the aircraft crashed into the sea opposite the River Annan. Its crew did not survive and only a wheel from the aircraft was found floating in the sea.

Date 31 August 1943
Aircraft H Hurricane
Location Silloth
Reference 165548
Aircrew –
This unidentified aircraft made a crash-landing on a sand bank a mile north-east of Silloth, following an engine failure. The station records did not identify the aircraft involved.

Date 2 September 1943
Aircraft M Martinet T1
Location Silloth
Reference 166549
Aircrew –
A mechanical failure caused the pilot to make a forced landing a mile north-east of RAF Silloth. The crew were unhurt and the plane was recovered a short time later. Again the identity of the aircraft was not noted.

Date 3 September 1943
Aircraft B Beaufort Mk I DX132
Location Longtown
Reference 405693
Aircrew Sgt JAL Grant 1394875
During a training flight from its base at RAF Longtown, this aircraft crashed killing its pilot at Hallburn. The wreckage was removed by a salvage unit a short time later.

Date 9 September 1943
Aircraft Unknown
Location Abbeytown
Reference 150420
Aircrew –
A police report details an aircraft making a forced landing in a field at Abbeytown, Aspatria. The crew were unhurt and the wreckage

removed by a crash team, its type and serial number not recorded.

Date 11 September 1943
Aircraft V Wellington (48)
Location Silloth
Reference 126542
Aircrew –
After the undercarriage failed to operate, the pilot made a belly landing alongside the runway. The crew escaped unhurt, and the plane was recovered by a crash team. The aircraft was identified only by its tail number.

Date 14 September 1943
Aircraft B-17 Flying Fortress USAAF
Location Keswick
Reference 256297
Aircrew Diltz. Sodbury + eight others
The crew of ten lost their lives when this B-17 crashed into Skiddaw mountain near Randel Cragg. The aircraft was from the USAAF and was engaged on a training flight over the Lake District. For some time after the accident the large tailplane could be seen high on the fellside, until salvage teams removed most of the remains. A climb to this site will still reveal many parts from the aircraft.

Date 18 September 1943
Aircraft B Beaufort Mk I LS133
Location Kirkbride
Reference 230550
Aircrew –
The tail wheel of this aircraft collapsed during its take-off run. The underside of the aircraft was badly damaged but it was repaired on site and later returned into service.

Date 23 September 1943
Aircraft A Anson Mk I N9718
Location Millom
Reference 129781
Aircrew P/O L Scott-Gibson J27481,
Sgt DSW Deane 605479,
Sgt D Clayton 1288501,
Sgt W Dowling 1562767
The bodies of the crew from this aircraft were washed ashore over a number of months follow-

ing its crash into the sea off Haverigg. Practically nothing of the aircraft was recovered.

Date	2 October 1943
Aircraft	L Hudson
Location	Silloth
Reference	126542
Aircrew	–

Failure of its starboard engine caused the aircraft to crash on the airfield. Its crew were unhurt and the aircraft was removed by a salvage unit. The aircraft's serial number was not recorded.

Date	10 October 1943
Aircraft	V Warwick Mk I BV415
Location	Kirkbride
Reference	230550
Aircrew	–

An hydraulic fault caused the undercarriage to collapse as the aircraft was taxying on the airfield. The crew were unhurt and the aircraft was repaired on site.

Date	11 October 1943
Aircraft	M Martinet TT1 JN657
Location	Grune Point
Reference	140570
Aircrew	–

An engine failure caused the pilot to crash-land on the mud flats at Grune Point. The crew escaped unhurt after the landing but the propeller was buried deep in the mud. When salvage units reached the aircraft with flotation bags, they were unable to free the aircraft as the propeller was acting as an anchor in the mud. They went to work with hacksaws and freed the propeller just minutes before the tide came in covering the area. This aircraft is on record as being the first to be recovered from the Solway Firth.

Date	14 October 1943
Aircraft	A Anson Mk I R9780
Location	Whitehaven
Reference	970170
Aircrew	F/O HJ O'Gara RAFVR 125569,
	Sgt S Johnston,
	Sgt T Inman RNFVR 1239963,
	Sgt VJ Dunningan RCAF r152072,
	Sgt RH Murphy RACF r151321

Few aircraft crashed on towns or villages, how-

ever this aircraft was seen to break up in mid-air over Whitehaven. Some of its crew of five tried to bale out but their parachutes failed to open because of their low height. Although the crew died there were no civilian casualties as the aircraft crashed onto the town.

Date	20 October 1943
Aircraft	HP Hampden Mk I P2113
Location	Westnewton
Reference	150450
Aircrew	ATA Flight Captain JE Martines

Shortly after one in the afternoon this aircraft crashed in a field near Westnewton and burst into flames. The pilot escaped from the burning wreck. He then returned to the aircraft to turn off the fuel cocks and began to fight the fire with a hand extinguisher. A short time later a crash team from RAF Kirkbride arrived on site and secured the aircraft until it was recovered. This ATA pilot was commended for his actions following the crash, caused by the failure of both the starboard and port engines.

Date	26 October 1943
Aircraft	H Hurricane Mk IIc LE262
Location	St Bees Head
Reference	988125
Aircrew	–

The pilot of this aircraft was killed and the aircraft destroyed after it crashed into a small hill between St Bees and Cleator. At the time of the accident the pilot was seen flying below the limits set for flying in cloud.

Date	10 November 1943
Aircraft	H Hurricane Mk XII JS392
Location	Silloth
Reference	126542
Aircrew	–

This aircraft was repaired on site and returned into service. It had crashed onto the taxi track after its undercarriage collapsed.

Date	13 November 1943
Aircraft	H Hurricane Mk I Z4875 55 OTU
Location	Cockermouth
Reference	148352
Aircrew	P/O RP Dixon 150191

This aircraft crashed at Milestone, near Moota. It

was on a training flight from its base at RAF Annan. Its pilot was killed and the wreckage was removed by a salvage unit.

Date	14 November 1943
Aircraft	B Beaufighter Mk VIc EL444
	9 OTU
Location	Dearham Bridge
Reference	067369
Aircrew	Sgt Glouster

Local people saw this aircraft hedge hopping across the fields shortly before it crashed near Dearham Bridge railway station. The wreckage was removed by a salvage team.

Date	15 November 1943
Aircraft	B Beaufighter Mk VIc EL285
	9 OTU
Location	Wolf Craggs
Reference	352225
Aircrew	Sgt IS Sollows r139005, Sgt MJ Lahausso 1515183

A large number of remains from this aircraft can still be seen amid the rocks at this site. It had crashed there while on a night operations training flight.

Date	16 November 1943
Aircraft	B Beaufighter Mk VIc JL814
Location	Crosby
Reference	480605
Aircrew	–

This pilot made a belly landing on the airfield at RAF Crosby following an engine failure. The crew were unhurt and the aircraft was later repaired on site and returned into service.

Date	17 November 1943
Aircraft	B Beaufort Mk I JM448
Location	Crosby
Reference	230550
Aircrew	–

Swinging off the runway during take-off, the undercarriage of this aircraft collapsed. Its crew

Remains from Beaufighter EL285 on Wolf Craggs. (MJ Hurst)

were unhurt and the aircraft returned into service following repair.

Date 19 November 1943
Aircraft B Beaufort Mk I JM583
Location Little Brampton
Reference 259559
Aircrew F/Lt AS Bancroft 88239,
F/O HE Joyce 151443,
F/O JWA Armstrong 151134

Two crew died as this aircraft crashed into the ground near Little Brampton, a third was released from the wreckage but died later in hospital. The wreckage was removed by a salvage unit.

Date 20 November 1943
Aircraft HP Halifax
Location Crosby
Reference 480605
Aircrew –

Following a serious mechanical failure in flight, the pilot ordered most of his crew to abandon the aircraft. He continued with his co-pilot and made a successful landing at RAF Crosby, meanwhile his crew all landed safely and were collected from the surrounding area.

Date 23 November 1943
Aircraft B-17 Flying Fortress 9913
USAAF
Location Millom
Reference 154820
Aircrew F/O PJ O'Sullivan USAAF
740532, F/O RL Garkie T707

This aircraft was one of five which had left the USA being delivered to the UK by their crews. Each aircraft made a stop over in Ireland to refuel and then continued to their destinations. This aircraft made an approach to RAF Haverigg in very poor weather conditions flying very low over the airfield. It continued on over Millom almost hitting the chimneys of the steel works heading off into low cloud, a few moments later there was a loud explosion. The bomber had crashed into High Low Scales where it exploded killing its crew. Wreckage from the aircraft could be seen from all over Millom for many weeks until it was removed by recovery units.

Date 29 November 1943
Aircraft DH Tiger Moth Mk II DE531
Location Kirkbride
Reference 230550
Aircrew –

Taxying too fast downwind the pilot collided with a tractor on the airfield. He was unhurt and the aircraft was later repaired on site.

Date 30 November 1943
Aircraft V Wellington
Location Silloth
Reference 126542
Aircrew –

This crew escaped unhurt after the aircraft overshot the runway on landing. It was badly damaged and later the same day recovered by crash teams.

Date 1 December 1943
Aircraft B Beaufighter Mk Ic T5108
Location Crosby
Reference 480605
Aircrew –

The undercarriage of this aircraft collapsed while landing, it crashed onto its belly and suffered what was described as medium damage. The crew were unhurt and following repairs the aircraft returned into service.

Date 2 December 1943
Aircraft HP Hampden Mk I TB P4347
Location Kirkbride
Reference 230550
Aircrew F/O Murthga

Being taxied around the airfield the plane was in collision with a concrete post and was badly damaged. It was later repaired and returned into service.

Date 3 December 1943
Aircraft B Beaufort Mk I JM584
Location Kirkbride
Reference 230550
Aircrew –

While making an engineless glide to the runway, the aircraft lost airspeed, stalled and crashed down onto the runway. It was badly damaged but its crew escaped with only minor injuries.

Date 8 December 1943
Aircraft B Beaufighter Mk X KW286
Location Kirkbride
Reference 230550
Aircrew –
An hydraulic failure in the braking system caused this aircraft to crash on the runway while landing. Its crew were unhurt and it was later returned into service following repair.

Date 9 December 1943
Aircraft B Beaufighter Mk I LZ146
Location Silloth
Reference 197558
Aircrew F/Sgt JW Boilstone 1245319
Following a stall while landing, the aircraft crashed at Marsh Farm, Newton Arlosh. Its pilot was killed and the aircraft burned out. The wreckage was removed by a salvage team.

Date 18 December 1943
Aircraft V Wellington (50)
Location Silloth
Reference 126542
Aircrew –
A failure of the port engine caused the pilot to make an emergency landing on the airfield, as he did the undercarriage collapsed. Its crew escaped unhurt and the aircraft was later repaired on site. This information was recorded in the station's log, but the aircraft was identified only by its unit marking.

Date 20 December 1943
Aircraft F Barracuda Mk II P9828 747 Sqd
Location High Arnside
Reference 021333
Aircrew Sub Lt GF Hopewell,
WHR Young RNVR, D Buttery
This aircraft crashed only a short distance from High Arnside House, near Coniston. The aircraft exploded on impact killing its crew of three and opened up a large crater. They were taking part in a night navigation training exercise from their base at RNAS Inskipp at the time of the accident. The majority of the wreckage was removed, but odd bits and pieces have been found near the crash site.

Date 28 December 1943
Aircraft H Hurricane Mk I V7010
55 OTU
H Hurricane Mk I AG175
55 OTU
Location Dalston
Reference 360515 / 365515
Aircrew P/O SF Cleworth j27208,
F/Sgt OE Louden NZ427044
Both pilots were killed following a mid-air collision. The aircraft crashed near Dalston. Rescue teams were quickly at the scene but could do little. One aircraft had buried itself in a deep crater and burned for two days, preventing the rescue teams from reaching the pilot. Most of the wreckage was removed but many parts were earthed over in the crater.

Date 31 December 1943
Aircraft B Beaufighter Mk VI KW152
Location Bootle Fell
Reference 145835
Aircrew F/Lt HS Ray 104522,
P/O JP Angold 47089
A number of pieces from this aircraft have been found at its crash site on Bootle Fell. Its crew died in the explosion which followed the impact.

Date 24 January 1944
Aircraft HP Halifax Mk II JP182
Location Eel Cragg
Reference 191211
Aircrew ATA Flight Captain B Short,
Eng A Bird
Piloted by an ATA crew, this aircraft struck the top of Eel Cragg above Keswick and exploded, having left RAF Silloth a short time earlier. Wreckage was scattered over a wide area and many parts can still be located.

Date 24 January 1944
Aircraft B Beaufighter Mk If T4772
Location Bewcastle
Reference 575780
Aircrew Sqd Ldr DN Milligan DFC 40553
The pilot of this aircraft was killed when his aircraft exploded after flying into the fellside at the 'Gew'. Parts from the aircraft can still be located at the crash site.

A hatch cover from Halifax bomber JP182 was found among wreckage at the Eel Cragg crash site. (MJ Hurst)

Date 25 January 1944
Aircraft V Wellington Mk XIV NB686
Location Silloth
Reference 126542
Aircrew –

Crash teams recovered this aircraft after it overshot the runway following a failure of its braking system. It crashed beyond the perimeter track. The accident was caused by failure of the starboard engine hydraulic pump. Its crew were unhurt.

Date 4 February 1944
Aircraft B Beaufighter Mk VIc JL774
Location Crosby
Reference 480605
Aircrew –

Just after the aircraft touched down at RAF Crosby, its port engine failed and the aircraft swung off the runway and crashed. Crash teams helped the uninjured but shaken crew from the wreckage.

Date 5 February 1944
Aircraft V Wellington
V Wellington
Location Silloth
Reference 126542
Aircrew –

These two accidents occurred within a short time of each other. Both aircraft were on a night flying exercise and both overshot the runway when landing and crashed in soft ground beyond. Neither of the crews was hurt and crash teams recovered the aircraft the following day. The account was taken from the station diary, but the aircrafts' identities were not recorded.

Date 14 February 1944
Aircraft HP Halifax Mk II BB278 1674 HCU
Location Solway Firth
Reference 126542
Aircrew P/O J Collinson 168979, Sgt
W Bostock 1032947, Sgt Izzard
578635, RA Olson j23786,
CJ Ballard 157082 and three
others.

The crew of this aircraft were killed when their Halifax from RAF Longtown crashed in the Solway Firth at Morecambe Bay and sank. Little was recovered from the aircraft and it still lies in the sands.

Date 18 February 1944
Aircraft V Wellington Mk Ic HE747
6c OTU
Location Silloth
Reference 126542
Aircrew Sgt E Malicki p784424 PAF,
F/Sgt A Kolkowsi

A few minutes before four in the afternoon, this aircraft was approaching to land at RAF Silloth. It was seen to stall and crash five miles south of the runway. One crew member was killed instantly, another died later in hospital. The remaining crew were all badly injured. Crash recovery teams removed the wreckage of the aircraft a few days later.

Date 19 February 1944
Aircraft B Beaufort Mk I L9948
9 OTU
Location Crosby
Reference 480605
Aircrew –

The undercarriage of this aircraft collapsed following a violent swing on the runway just after the aircraft had landed. Its crew were unhurt and the aircraft was recovered by a crash team.

Date 20 February 1944
Aircraft B Beaufighter Mk Vc JL570
Location Crosby
Reference 480605
Aircrew –

While making a circuit of the airfield one of the aircraft's engines failed. Shortly afterwards the second engine failed and the pilot made a belly landing on the airfield. Its crew were unhurt and the aircraft was recovered by a crash team.

Date 21 February 1944
Aircraft V Wellington Mk III BK506
9 OTU
Location Cliburn
Reference 588258
Aircrew Sgt MP Proteu CANR 214121,
Sgt PP Medderick CANR 214141

While flying from RAF Pershore to RAF Crosby, the aircraft was seen circling near Penrith. It had got into difficulties during the flight and was trying to locate a satellite airfield near Penrith. Unable to maintain height the aircraft crashed near Cliburn, close to the satellite landing ground. Risking their own lives as a bomb bay of burning incendiary devices was exploding around them, airmen from the satellite airfield helped the crew escape from the burning wreckage. One crew member died in the accident and the remaining survivors were taken to a nearby farmhouse to await transportation to hospital.

Date 23 February 1944
Aircraft V Wellington Mk III BK156
Location Solway Firth
Reference 948267
Aircrew P/O JJ Zywicki p2523

En route from RAF Bircotes this aircraft ditched into the sea off Workington. Air-sea rescue boats managed to save all the crew with the exception of the navigator who could not be found. His body was recovered from the sea the following day.

Date 25 February 1944
Aircraft B Beaufighter Mk Ic T5106
9 OTU
Location Crosby
Reference 480605
Aircrew –

Shortly after landing the aircraft's undercarriage collapsed. The aircraft was subsequently returned into service following repair. The crew were unhurt.

Date 25 February 1944
Aircraft B Beaufighter Mk VIc X8070
Location Crosby
Reference 480605
Aircrew –

This aircraft's undercarriage also collapsed on landing the same day. Another repair on site with the aircraft returning into service.

Date 8 March 1944
Aircraft B Beaufort Mk I L4457 9 OTU
Location Crosby
Reference 480605
Aircrew –

This aircraft landed heavily, bounced, its starboard wing and dropped, hitting the runway. The engine caught fire and within seconds its undercarriage collapsed causing the aircraft to crash to the ground. The crew escaped unhurt and crash teams dealt with the aircraft, which was later removed by a salvage unit.

Date 10 March 1944
Aircraft B Beaufighter Mk 6 JM115 9 OTU
Location Crosby
Reference 480605
Aircrew –
An engine failure after take-off was the cause of this accident. The pilot tried to land back on the runway but overshot. The aircraft crashed in soft ground at the end of the runway.

Date 11 March 1944
Aircraft B Beaufighter Mk Ic T4712
9 OTU
B Beaufighter Mk Ic T4655
9 OTU
Location Crosby
Reference 480605
Aircrew –
Both aircraft collided on the runway while trying to take off together. Their crews were unhurt and the aircraft were recovered by crash teams.

Date 13 March 1944
Aircraft B Beaufighter Mk 6c T5271
9 OTU
Location Crosby
Reference 480605
Aircrew –
Following a failure of the aircraft's starboard engine during take-off, the pilot was forced to make an emergency landing. The aircraft was slightly damaged and repaired on site, returning into service a short time later.

Date 18 March 1944
Aircraft M Martinet TT I HP274
Location Firbank Fell, Mossfoot
Reference 618923
Aircrew Sgt TH Allan 1561236
Poor visibility and deteriorating weather were the cause of this accident. The aircraft crashed on Firbank Fell killing its pilot. Wreckage was scattered over a wide area and wrapped around the wreckage and rocks was the long steel cable used by the aircraft when towing targets.

Date 20 March 1944
Aircraft H Hurricane Mk I AF970 3 TEU
Location Castle Carrock
Reference 542555
Aircrew F/Sgt JH Broad r153684
A routine training flight ended when the aircraft crashed near Castle Carrock killing its pilot. The wreckage was removed by a salvage unit.

Date 20 March 1944
Aircraft A Anson Mk I EG686 25 SPTU
VS Spitfire unidentified
Location Coniston
Reference 276988
Aircrew (Anson) Sgt KM Snelling + two
others
This crash site is less than one mile from the Halifax bomber on Great Carrs, but is not as well known. Many large sections of this aircraft can be located on the southern slopes of Swirl How and in the small stream at the bottom. Both engines can still be seen, cadets from Windermere ATC recovered one of the propellers in 1974. The aircraft had been heading for RAF Cark but lost radio contact over the Irish Sea. When the aircraft became overdue a search operation commenced. The wreckage of the Anson was finally spotted by a search aircraft midway up Swirl How. Crash teams were dispatched to the scene. The mountain rescue unit which went to this aircraft also found a Spitfire close by with its dead pilot still inside. It had crashed into level ground and overturned breaking its pilot's neck. Damage to the aircraft was slight and it was dismantled and returned to RAF Cark. It was rebuilt and flown on air test after repair by the station commander. No record of the aircraft or the identity of its pilot could be found during our research and it remains unknown. It is believed that it crashed over a month prior to the Anson accident. Details of both incidents were provided by the then Commanding Officer of RAF Cark.

Still complete with its tyre is the undercarriage of Anson EG686 below the summit of Coniston Old Man. (MJ Hurst)

Date 31 March 1944
Aircraft B Beaufort Mk I L9963 9 OTU
Location Crosby
Reference 480605
Aircrew –
Following a bad landing on Crosby airfield, the undercarriage failed causing the plane to crash. It was later repaired on site and returned into service.

Date 31 March 1944
Aircraft B Beaufighter Mk II JM128
Location Crosby
Reference 480605
Aircrew –

Accidents at Crosby seem to come in two's. This aircraft's engines failed, its undercarriage collapsed and the plane was quite badly damaged. It returned into service following repair.

Date 6 April 1944
Aircraft V Wellington Mk 12 MP682
6c OTU
Location Solway Firth
Reference 115582
Aircrew Sgt EA Dempsey 1494695
The wireless operator of this aircraft died after his aircraft crashed into the Solway Firth. The

remaining crew survived, being able to escape from the aircraft as it sank.

Date 6 April 1944
Aircraft B Beaufighter Mk 6c T5349
Location Crosby
Reference 480605
Aircrew –

Following an engine failure in flight the pilot made a crash-landing on the airfield. The crew were unhurt and crash teams recovered the aircraft.

Date 9 April 1944
Aircraft B Beaufighter Mk 6c T5104
Location Crosby
Reference 48605
Aircrew –

This accident occurred because the undercarriage failed to lock down. The crew escaped unhurt though the aircraft was badly damaged.

Date 9 April 1944
Aircraft B Beaufighter Mk 6c JL820
Location Great Orton
Reference 326538
Aircrew –

The pilot of this aircraft forgot to set the fuel transfer switches and a crash-landing resulted as the engines failed. Crash teams were quickly on site to assist the pilot, who was unhurt.

Date 12 April 1944
Aircraft HP Halifax Mk II BB310
1674 HCU 17 Grp
Location Blea Cragg
Reference 694324
Aircrew F/Sgt GS Johnson 1107720,
DW Swidberg, F Press,
GB Harkness, S Brooks,
SH Seabrook, RJ Likefield,
H Dunningham,
WJ Morrison

Beneath Cross Fell on the western slopes are the remains of this Halifax bomber which crashed into Blea Cragg. Its crew of nine died in the explosion which followed, and wreckage was scattered over a wide area. Many parts can be found and much was melted from the intense heat from the fire. A large burn scar can also be seen at the crash site.

Date 13 April 1944
Aircraft B Beaufighter Mk Ic T5103 9
(c) OTU
A Anson Mk I DJ564
Location Solway Firth
Reference 078493 / 094518
Aircrew W/O2 JK Gillies r146737, F/O T
Sandberg j24115

A mechanical failure forced the Anson's pilot to ditch in the sea off Blackshaw Bank. Air-sea rescue boats set out to try and locate the aircraft but daylight was fading. As night approached search aircraft flew over the area dropping flares to assist the boats in their search. One of these was a Beaufighter from RAF Crosby which after dropping its flares suffered a double engine failure and crashed into the sea. The rescue boats were diverted to find the Beaufighter, but its crew had also been killed. Both aircraft sank. The aircraft had been involved in an accident at RAF Crosby in January 1943.

Date 16 April 1944
Aircraft B Beaufighter Mk X KW293
9 OTU
Location Caldbeck
Reference 297423
Aircrew Sgt G Torres ff30714, Sgt Ash

On a training flight from its base this aircraft crashed at Hill Top near Caldbeck killing its pilot and injuring its navigator. Some wreckage can still be located at the crash site.

Date 19 April 1944
Aircraft V Wellington Mk XIV HF ???
Location Unknown
Reference Unknown
Aircrew –

Other than a report of this aircraft being lost over the Lake District, no other information is known. Only the first letters of the aircraft serial number were recorded in the police account of the incident.

Date 23 April 1944
Aircraft B Beaufighter Mk 6c T5108
Location Crosby
Reference 528628
Aircrew –
The crew of this aircraft escaped with minor injuries when a mechanical failure resulted in it crashing two miles north-east of the airfield. Crash teams removed the aircraft a few days later.

Date 27 April 1944
Aircraft B Beaufighter Mk 6c T5217
Location Silloth
Reference 160554
Aircrew –
While taking part in a low-level air firing exercise, a double engine failure caused the pilot to make a crash-landing on a marsh three miles north of the airfield. The crew escaped unhurt and salvage teams recovered the wreckage.

Date 2 May 1944
Aircraft M Martinet
Location Seascale
Reference 034020
Aircrew –
A twenty-year-old ATC Cadet was working in a field near Seascale when he saw the Martinet crash-land in the adjacent field and burst into flames. One occupant was thrown clear of the aircraft but the pilot was trapped in the cockpit. The cadet ran to the aircraft, freed the pilot and managed to pull him clear before the flames engulfed the cockpit. Later in the year, he was awarded the British Empire Medal for his act of bravery.

Cam Spout and the surrounding fell were searched for the remains of A Anson DJ275.
(MJ Hurst)

Date 4 May 1944
Aircraft B Beaufighter Mk 6c JM127
Location Crosby
Reference 480605
Aircrew –
Following a normal landing, the starboard under-carriage collapsed, causing the aircraft to swing from the runway and crash. Its crew were unhurt and repairs were later carried out on site.

Date 29 May 1944
Aircraft M Martinet B129
Location Crosby
Reference 480605
Aircrew –
After a normal landing, one of the aircraft's tyres burst. It swung from the runway and overturned causing extensive damage. Its pilot escaped unhurt. The aircraft was identified by its wing number.

Date 16 June 1944
Aircraft V Wellington Mk X HZ715 22 OTU
Location Keswick
Reference 159154
Aircrew P/O AD Cooper j18201,
F/O F Dixon, F/Lt E Unterseher j1629, P/O D Titleman,
W/O GR Coathup, F/O RF Simonson, Sgt CM Hodges,
Sgt GM Anderson
Wreckage from this aircraft can still be found on the slopes of Red Pike. The eight crew on board this aircraft died as it crashed into the mountain and exploded. The aircraft was flying from RAF Wellesbourne Mountford in Warwickshire on a cross-country navigation exercise when the accident occurred.

Date 17 June 1944
Aircraft B Beaufighter Mk II JM173
Location Askerton
Reference 583692
Aircrew F/O EF Keefe 139974, F/O A Dey 152955
Wreckage from this aircraft was scattered over a wide area when it crashed killing its crew near Askerton Castle Farm. Salvage units recovered

the wreckage a few days later but some items have been seen at the crash site.

Date 19 June 1944
Aircraft B Beaufighter Mk 6c JL572 9c OTU
Location Crosby
Reference 480605
Aircrew –
While making an approach to the runway, the starboard wing dropped, coming into contact with the ground. The pilot managed to recover and made another circuit and a second approach. As the aircraft touched down, its undercarriage collapsed and the aircraft crashed down onto the runway. The crew escaped unhurt and a salvage team recovered the wreckage.

Date 26 June 1944
Aircraft V Wellington Mk X HF155
Location Silloth
Reference 126542
Aircrew –
RAF Silloth was placed on a full alert as this aircraft came into land on fire carrying a full load of depth charges. It crashed 400 yards short of the runway and erupted in flames. The aircraft was totally destroyed as the depth charges exploded.

Date 6 July 1944
Aircraft B Beaufighter Mk II JL945 9 OTU
Location Silloth
Reference 126542
Aircrew –
A routine training flight which ended with an emergency landing caused by an engine failure. There was no damage to either crew or aircraft.

Date 6 July 1944
Aircraft B Beaufighter Mk VIc JL825
Location Crosby
Reference 480605
Aircrew –
Another undercarriage failure after the aircraft swung from the runway while landing. Damage to the aircraft was repaired on site and the aircraft later returned into service.

Date 23 July 1944
Aircraft B Beaufighter Mk II JM163
Location Crosby
Reference 480605
Aircrew –
This aircraft blew a tyre on take-off following which the pilot made a belly landing. Its crew were unhurt although the aircraft was badly damaged.

Date 28 July 1944
Aircraft M Martinet Mk I HP311
Location High Duddon
Reference 190894
Aircrew P/O FL Dumbleton 177685
Crash and rescue units from RAF Haverigg attended this aircraft after it crashed near High Duddon killing its pilot. The majority of the wreckage was removed by salvage units. The serial number recorded in this accident was not allocated to a Martinet, making confirmation of the aircraft uncertain.

Date 3 August 1944
Aircraft V Wellington Mk X HF470
Location Cark
Reference 395748
Aircrew –
Part way through a training flight this aircraft was diverted to RAF Cark from its base at RAF Silloth. After a short stay, it was taking off to return to Silloth when it suffered an engine failure. The aircraft overshot the run-way, crashed through a hedge and into a hut. Its crew were unhurt but the plane was badly damaged.

Date 25 August 1944
Aircraft M Martinet
Location Solway Firth
Reference 100550
Aircrew F/Sgt Gowdie 538595,
LAC Hunter
The crew of two were killed after the aircraft crashed into the Solway Firth and sank. Their bodies and some of the wreckage were recovered a short time later. The station log did not record the aircraft's serial number.

Date 14 September 1944
Aircraft V Wellington Mk X HF200
6(c) OTU
Location Silloth
Reference 126542
Aircrew W/O RA Davies 1219225, Sgt
JHW Durrant 1333947,
LAC N Stott 1697788
Three crew from this aircraft died as it crashed onto Silloth airfield. No other details of the accident are recorded.

Date 16 September 1944
Aircraft V Wellington Mk X HF179
Location Solway Firth
Reference 182105
Aircrew F/Lt LWH Coe 120942,
F/O GE Lumley 171707,
P/O HC Waters,
F/O OJ Lander 55093
In the sea off St Bees Head are the remains of this aircraft which was ditched during a training flight with the loss of four crew. Little was recovered from the aircraft.

Date 29 September 1944
Aircraft Unknown
Location Silecroft
Reference Unknown
Aircrew –
Details of this accident are sparse, all that was confirmed in a police report was that the crew of a ditched aircraft were rescued by an air-sea rescue launch off Silecroft in the afternoon.

Date 15 October 1944
Aircraft HP Halifax BB116 109 OTU
Location Marvins Pike
Reference 569872
Aircrew –
Four crew were killed as this aircraft crashed into Marvins Pike near Glendue Hill in the late evening.The aircraft was from RAF Standcroft taking part in an exercise. Most of the wreckage was removed by salvage teams although some parts have been found at the site.

Date 17 October 1944
Aircraft HP Halifax Mk VII NP745
408 Sqd 6 Grp
Location Penruddock
Reference 429278
Aircrew F/O JE Freeman j39402, F/O JE
Austin j24625, F/Sgt JC Mortley
r175266, Sgt TH Chandler
1594677, P/O CL Johnston j89128

A combination of poor weather and low fuel forced the crew of this aircraft to bale out near Ullswater, all landed safely with only one crew member suffering minor injuries. The aircraft, however, flew on until it crashed in a field near the centre of Penruddock village. The impact blew off slates, broke windows and started many small fires, wreckage from the aircraft was scattered over a wide area. Fire and crash units attended the accident and it took a number of weeks to remove the wreckage and repair the damage. Some of the wreckage was buried in the ground near a small stream, where at least one engine is known to remain in the ground today. The aircraft was from RAF Linton on Ouse in Yorkshire.

Date 22 October 1944
Aircraft HP Halifax Mk V LL505
1659 HCU 6 Grp
Location Coniston
Reference 271008
Aircrew F/O JA Johnson,
Sgt WB Ferguson, Sgt HE Pychem,
Sgt CG Whittingstall,
F/O FA Bell, P/O RN Whitley,
Sgt DF Titt, Sgt G Riddoch

This is probably the most well known and visited crash site in the Lake District. Many large sections of the aircraft can still be found on the scree slopes and in the gullies including all four of the aircraft's engines. The aircraft crashed on the top of Great Carrs, killing its crew of eight Canadians. When discovered the aircraft was almost intact. Crash teams faced with the impossible task of removing the aircraft from this location cut the aircraft into sections and pushed them into Broad Slack. This was done to prevent the aircraft crash site being repeatedly reported. The aircraft was on a night navigation training flight from its base at RAF Topcliffe.

Date 1 November 1944
Aircraft V Wellington Mk XII MP680
6c OTU
Location Silloth
Reference 126542
Aircrew Sgt J Thomas 1650201,
P/O NH Goodwin 182007,
F/Sgt J Land 1431070, Sgt Bull,
Sgt Kury, Sgt Dowse

Little else is known other than the fact that this aircraft crashed on the airfield killing its crew of six.

Date 14 November 1944
Aircraft DH Tiger Moth Mk II T6828
15 EFTS
Location Bewcastle
Reference 561855
Aircrew Sgt FES Plamer 1808685,
Sgt RM Medwin 11808235

Crash teams had difficulty recovering the bodies of the crew from this aircraft after it crashed on Glen Due. The aircraft was completely destroyed and the majority of the wreckage was removed or buried. It was discovered on the sixteenth following a large-scale search.

Date 17 November 1944
Aircraft A Anson Mk I MG464 AN & B
29 Grp
Location Keswick
Reference 198218
Aircrew Sgt RW Bradford

The following is the pilot's own account of this accident:

On the night of 17 November 1944, I was the pilot of an Avro Anson Mk I, identified in my log book as SI and assigned the call letter 'J'. I was engaged in a night flying exercise from RAF Station Jurby, Isle of Man, carrying a crew of three. Records will show that the weather was poor with some possibility of cumulus nimbus in the Lake District. To make a long story shorter, I hit severe turbulence in the squall end of a cumulus nimbus thunder head and lost considerable height in the downdraft. Two other aircraft in the exercise hit the central updraft and were thrown clear out of the head at a greater altitude without structural failure. I fell into

The author and his crash team examine the wreckage of the fuselage from Halifax LL505 on Great Carrs. This was one of the largest wreck sites in the Lake District. Much has now been removed by souvenir hunters. (The Observer)

Planning the search of Long Cragg for Anson MG464. This search took four days. (MJ Hurst)

a valley near the village of Braithwaite and during my climb out in rain and darkness I managed to miss one ridge of high ground only to hit the next at about 9.15 p.m. Later RCAF correspondence with my father indicated that I crashed on Long Craggs near Braithwaite.

Although difficult to locate, quite an amount of wreckage remains at the crash site.

Date 27 November 1944
Aircraft DH Mosquito Mk 5 BVI NT147 3FPP
Location Kirkbride
Reference 230550
Aircrew 3rd Off JF Wheelock
An ATA pilot was killed when this aircraft crashed onto RAF Kirkbride airfield. Little other information on the accident was recorded.

Date 1 December 1944
Aircraft VS Spitfire Mk V EP518
Location Askerton
Reference 580730
Aircrew Sgt B Zeman 1777554
After crashing into Side Fell, Askerton, the aircraft exploded killing its pilot. Most of the wreckage was removed but some parts have been seen in the area.

Date 6 December 1944
Aircraft D Dakota Mk III KG639
Location Unknown
Reference Unknown
Aircrew P/O Heyes
Little information is recorded on this accident other than an entry in the Register of Deaths. The aircraft crashed killing its pilot. The exact location was not recorded.

Date 6 December 1944
Aircraft V Wellington Mk XII HF199
Location Cold Fell
Reference 604555
Aircrew F/O J Sheldon 173551

Taking part in a night flying exercise, this aircraft crashed on Cold Fell killing its crew of five and a flying instructor. The accident occurred in poor weather. Although a large portion of wreckage was removed some sections were buried on site.

Date 27 December 1944
Aircraft DH Tiger Moth
Location Kingstown
Reference 392594
Aircrew –
This aircraft crashed while on take-off. Its undercarriage was ripped off and the upper wing damaged as it turned over onto its back. The log did not record the aircraft's serial number.

Date 2 January 1945
Aircraft A Anson Mk I T7411
Location Corney Fell
Reference 140859
Aircrew W/O TW Johnson 1526829, F/Sgt AF Wood 1318079, F/Sgt H Bitten, Sgt JL Turner 1823803, Sgt DK Jenkins 1836729
A hundred feet below the summit of Black Combe are the remains of this aircraft which crashed killing its crew of five. The aircraft was reported missing on a flight from RAF Jurby to RAF Haverigg. One of its crew that day was reported as the Commanding Officer of Haverigg; however, there is some confusion surrounding the report of this accident, as the serial number was not issued to this aircraft type. The rank of the aircrew listed would not be those expected of a station commander.

Date 8 January 1945
Aircraft A Anson Mk I EF935 10 AFU
Location Corney Fell
Reference 136926
Aircrew W/O H Biffin 1336043
Another Anson and the same area as the previous crash. One crew member was killed and three others were injured after this aircraft also hit Corney Fell. The majority of the wreckage was either removed or buried at the site by the salvage units, though some parts can still be located.

A search of Corney Fell is undertaken by cadets from 1264 Sqd Air Training Corps. Their objective is to find Anson EF935. (MJ Hurst)

Date	16 January 1945
Aircraft	G Avenger Mk II JZ390 763 Sqd
Location	Wastwater
Reference	148039
Aircrew	Lt BJ Kennedy RCNVR, AG Fell RNVR, P Royston-Mallorie

Flying from its base at RNAS Inskipp on a night training flight the aircraft flew into a steep scree slope at the side of Wastwater. The crew of three were killed and the aircraft broke up scattering wreckage down the slopes, some of which lies in the water today. A walk along the shore path will lead you to the large Wright Cyclone radial engine which is lying at the water's edge. Other parts of the aircraft can be seen among the rocks in gullies between Whin Rigg and Illgill Head. An almost complete tail section was found on the lake bed by a local diving club.

Date	19 January 1945
Aircraft	DH Tiger Moth Mk II T5960 DH Tiger Moth Mk I N9160
Location	Unknown
Reference	Unknown
Aircrew	–

Remains of the Wright Cyclone engine from the G Avenger lying by the edge of Wastwater Lake. (MJ Hurst)

The location of these crash sites is unrecorded, although there is a record in the station log, and police reports of them being destroyed in a mid-air collision in the Lake District on the 19th.

Date	10 February 1945
Aircraft	DH Mosquito Mk NF12 HK141
Location	Ullswater
Reference	348157
Aircrew	Sgt CF Marshall Aus433705 RAAF, W/O WD Frost Aus420616 RAAF

This aircraft flying from RAF Cranfield hit the edge of Catstye Cam on Helvellyn. It flew on a short distance breaking up in flight and crashed onto Striding Edge. Its crew of two were killed and one engine from the aircraft rolled down the scree slope and onto the frozen surface of Red Tarn. Wreckage was scattered over a wide area and much can be seen in the rock field; other parts still remain at the bottom of the tarn.

Date	24 March 1945
Aircraft	V Wellington Mk X NC691
Location	Millom
Reference	125800
Aircrew	W/O NH Pinlington 1379350, W/O NF Rouse 954186

The crew of this aircraft lost their lives after it crashed into the sea off Haverigg. Little was recovered from the aircraft and the bodies of the crew were washed ashore some two months later.

Date	26 March 1945
Aircraft	DH Tiger Moth Mk II T5362
Location	Kingstown
Reference	392594
Aircrew	–

Crash teams rescued the pilot of this aircraft after he crashed on the airfield. He was taken to hospital for emergency treatment. Crash teams removed the aircraft.

Date	26 March 1945
Aircraft	NA Mustang
Location	Kingstown
Reference	392594
Aircrew	–

Flying from its base at RAF Digby, the pilot made a crash-landing on the airfield following an engine failure. He was unhurt and the aircraft was later repaired on site and returned into service.

Date	25 April 1945
Aircraft	L Mitchell Mk III KJ562
Location	Kirkbride
Reference	230550
Aircrew	F/Lt AL Davis

An engine failure caused the pilot of this aircraft to make an emergency landing on the airfield. The crew were unhurt and the aircraft was repaired on site. It returned into service a few days later.

Chapter Three

1945 to 1976

Date 7 May 1945
Aircraft DH Tiger Moth Mk II T6930
Location Unknown
Reference Unknown
Aircrew –

A report of this aircraft crashing was entered in police records, but no other information was available.

Date 31 May 1945
Aircraft Unknown
Location Unknown
Reference –
Aircrew –

Another report taken from police records, and an entry in the station diary, but no firm information was recorded. The aircraft was reported as having crashed in the Lake District.

Date 1 June 1945
Aircraft D Dakota Mk III KG633
Location Crosby
Reference –
Aircrew –

Following a normal landing the pilot taxied into a parked truck on the airfield. Both the truck and aircraft were badly damaged, the truck was scrapped and the aircraft later repaired on site.

Date 25 June 1945
Aircraft DH Tiger Moth Mk II DE215
7 PRC
Location Ullswater
Reference 415196
Aircrew Sgt IW Jenkins 1606639

This aircraft still lies in Ullswater after it crashed during a training flight. One of its crew managed to escape from the wreckage but the second crew member was drowned as the aircraft sank. Its exact location is uncertain now, and the reference refers to the position given by its pilot.

Date 1 July 1945
Aircraft NA Mustang
Location Crosthwaite
Reference 912445
Aircrew –

On a Saturday morning two Mustangs were flying from RAF Cark along the Lythe Valley when one aircraft developed engine problems. At about 10.30 a.m. residents reported seeing the aircraft overhead with one in obvious difficulties. It had black smoke coming from its engine and was also misfiring. The pilot appeared to be looking for somewhere to land the plane and began to circle the village. The aircraft hit the top of some trees behind the vicarage and then hit the vicarage roof, losing part of its wing. It then crashed down onto the lawn and roadway bursting into flames. As ammunition from the plane started to explode the landlord of the Punch Bowl Hotel and others ran to help the pilot; they had to cut his straps to free him and managed to pull him clear of the flames that now engulfed the cockpit. Unfortunately he had been killed in the impact and there was little else they could do. The second aircraft returned to Cark and its pilot visited his companion's crash site later that afternoon.

Date 24 July 1945
Aircraft M Martinet
Location Millom
Reference 129781
Aircrew –

During a training flight from RAF Walney Island, the aircraft suffered an engine failure. The crew baled out and came down in the sea near Millom. They were rescued by local boatmen and later taken to the station sick quarters at RAF Haverigg to recover. The aircraft remains in the sands off Millom.

Date 28 December 1945
Aircraft A Anson Mk I DJ441
Location Kingstown
Reference 392594
Aircrew –

Trains were brought to a halt after this aircraft ended up on the railway lines near Kingstown airfield. The aircraft had overshot the runway, crashed through a fence and across the perimeter track. The plane was on a training flight from its base at RAF Jurby. Its crew were unhurt and the aircraft was recovered by a salvage unit.

Date 31 December 1945
Aircraft D Dakota Mk 3 FL652 1338
(t) CU 4 Grp
Location Carlisle
Reference 480605
Aircrew –

The crew of this aircraft had a lucky escape after they crashed while landing and overshot the runway. They crashed into a line of flight huts and a fierce fire followed. Both service and civilian fire crews attended the accident.

Date 3 February 1946
Aircraft D Dakota Mk 3 KG502 1383
(t) CU 4 Grp
Location Carlisle
Reference 605548
Aircrew –

Taking part in a night flying exercise this aircraft crashed killing its crew on Cold Fell near Carlisle. Much of the wreckage was removed by salvage units though some was buried at the site and odd parts can still be located. Reports of the accident state that the aircraft was heard to circle Carlisle before the crash, the wings of the aircraft were ripped off in the impact and wreckage scattered over a wide area.

Date 19 March 1946
Aircraft Unidentified
Location Carlisle
Reference 405587
Aircrew –

An unidentified aircraft crashed into a small field near Hadrian's Camp, Carlisle. After landing it ran into a ditch and turned over. The forced landing was caused by an engine failure. The police report failed to record the aircraft type and identity.

Date 1 July 1946
Aircraft V Wellington Mk X LP764
10AGS 25Grp
Location Irish Sea
Reference 931308
Aircrew F/O R Gray, F/Lt Flower

An SOS was received from this aircraft which was carrying out an ammunition dumping flight over the Irish Sea flying from RAF Walney Island. The SOS advised that the pilot was about to ditch the aircraft into the sea just off the west coast. An intensive air-sea rescue operation was undertaken involving some thirty aircraft and ships; despite the search no trace of the aircraft or its crew was found.

Date 2 July 1946
Aircraft A Anson Mk I MG437 5 ANS
25 Grp
Location Irish Sea
Reference 932294
Aircrew –

The search for the missing Wellington bomber was continued the following day. This Anson was flying from RAF Jurby over the search area when it crashed into the mast of a fishing boat as it was climbing to pass over; one wing was ripped off and the aircraft crashed into the sea. The aircraft sank almost at once taking its crew with it. An extensive search for the crew began but no one was found.

Date 8 July 1946
Aircraft V Warwick Mk I ASR HF944 5FP
41 FPP
Location Silloth
Reference 149569
Aircrew –

The pilot of this aircraft was trying to make a forced landing on Silloth airfield after an engine developed problems. It was seen to turn onto its side and sideslip into the ground erupting in flames at Balladoyle Farm. When crash teams reached the aircraft they found the body of the pilot still tightly gripping the aircraft's controls.

The wreckage was removed by a salvage unit some time later.

Date 10 July 1946
Aircraft A Lancaster
Location Millom
Reference 195805
Aircrew –

The identity of this aircraft will probably not be known, and maybe the crew would prefer it that way. Local people saw it flying near Millom as if trying to locate its position, it then made a landing on flat sands opposite the town. One crew member jumped down from the aircraft and made his way to some local fishermen. He enquired of the location and then climbed back into the aircraft, which then took off and disappeared into the distance. They were in fact quite lucky as the sands in that area are notorious for being soft in places and are constantly shifting. Why they chose not to land on Haverigg airfield is not known, assuming of course that they had actually located it.

Date 30 August 1946
Aircraft DH Dominie 89a X7394 782 Sqd (RN)
Location Scafell
Reference 219078
Aircrew Slt SK Kilsby, CP/O HJ Clark, SC WMT Gwynne-Jones, LH Watkinson, CR Alright

This air ambulance was flying from Abbotsinch to Streeton when it crashed into Broad Cragg on Scafell. It struck the rock face three to four hundred feet below the summit and crashed down onto the scree slope and rocks below. After it became overdue an air search by RAF and RN aircraft was started to try and locate the plane. It was spotted by an Anson from RNAS Anthorn below the cragg. When rescue teams reached it they found the crew and its passenger dead near the wreckage. A visit to the site will still show many parts of the aircraft, including its engines.

Date 8 September 1946
Aircraft Foster Winker Wicko G-AFJB
Location North of Walney Island
Reference 210785
Aircrew –

An engine failure over the sea caused the pilot to head for land and attempt a forced landing. Trying to avoid a stone wall the aircraft hit it and overturned falling back onto the beach. The aircraft sank in the sea but its crew were unhurt. The aircraft is reported to have been salvaged and returned into service later in the year.

Date 11 November 1946
Aircraft F Argus F-24W-41A Mk 2 G-AITG
Location Silloth
Reference 210785
Aircrew F Bosworth

Leaving Silloth airfield for RAF White Waltham, a mechanical failure caused the aircraft to crash on the beach near North House. Salvage units removed the aircraft after a few days.

Date 20 December 1946
Aircraft V Wellington Mk II NC445
Location Kirkbride
Reference 230550
Aircrew –

Airborne from its base at Bishops Court, this aircraft was being delivered to the maintenance unit at Kirkbride. The aircraft overshot the runway while landing and crashed through the perimeter fence. Although badly damaged it was repaired on site and later returned into operational service.

Date 13 March 1947
Aircraft B C-45 Expeditor USAAF
Location Black Combe
Reference 135858
Aircrew Cpt J Daner, 1st Lt A Garner

En route from RAF Prestwick to RAF Bovingdon in Hertfordshire, the aircraft flew into a blizzard crossing the Solway Firth. The pilot carried on and then flew into a snowdrift on the side of Black Combe. The crew members survived in spite of being catapulted into the snowdrift; both spent a cold night in the aircraft cabin, wrapped in their parachutes. The following day they made their way down the fellside to Holeghyll Farm from where they were taken to a local hospital and treated for exposure and frostbite. Many large parts of this aircraft can still be seen at the crash site.

Date 19 June 1947
Aircraft M Martinet Mk I EM524 631 Sqd
12 Grp
Location Bigrigg
Reference 999136
Aircrew W/O A Bell, Cpl V King

During a routine training flight from its base at RAF Silloth a mechanical failure prompted a forced landing. The pilot chose a field near St John's Church at Bigrigg. As he came in to land the wing of the aircraft struck a tree and it spun into the ground, bursting into flames. What remained of the aircraft continued skidding across the ground breaking up as it went. The cockpit crossed a small road narrowly missing a van and ended up on the grass verge burning fiercely. The crew escaped unhurt but badly shaken. They were taken to hospital by the van driver, the local police placed a guard on the aircraft until it was removed by a salvage team.

Date 10 October 1947
Aircraft P Proctor LZ598
Location Silloth
Reference 210785
Aircrew –

Preparing for take-off the pilot taxied the aircraft too quickly, resulting in it overturning on the taxiway. The pilot was unhurt and repairs to the aircraft were carried out on the airfield.

Date 20 November 1947
Aircraft VS Spitfire Mk XVI SL611
603 Sqd
Location Ill Cragg
Reference 222075
Aircrew F/Lt DJO Loudon

Wreckage from this aircraft can still be seen at its crash site on Ill Cragg, Scafell, forty feet north-east of the summit cairn. It was reported missing on a flight from RAF Hullavington to its base at RAF Turnhouse. Despite an extensive air-sea rescue search the aircraft and the body of its pilot were not found until May 1948.

Date 9 March 1948
Aircraft VS Spitfire
Location Silloth
Reference 210785
Aircrew

Flying from RAF Brize Norton this aircraft blew a tyre on landing at Silloth. The aircraft ran onto the grass damaging its undercarriage. The pilot was unhurt and the aircraft was repaired on site.

Date 25 March 1948
Aircraft M Aerovan G-AJKT
Location Irish Sea
Reference 930323
Aircrew –

The pilot of this aircraft was rescued by a boat after ditching in the Irish Sea off Silecroft. The aircraft was en route from Ireland to Liverpool when it came down.

Date 9 May 1948
Aircraft M Messenger
M Geminie
Location Maryport / Winscales
Reference 054389 / 027088
Aircrew –

On delivery from Belfast to Liverpool, a fuel failure caused the pilot to make a forced landing on the golf links at Maryport. Repairs were carried out on site and the aircraft continued its journey. Luck was not with the aircraft as yet another mechanical failure caused the pilot to make another landing at Winscales. This time he was unable to carry out repairs and requested assistance. A Geminie aircraft left Belfast and brought spares and technical assistance to the luckless pilot. The Messenger was repaired by a mechanic and it left to continue its journey to Liverpool. As the Geminie and its crew left to return to Belfast, it crashed in an adjacent field. It was not possible to repair the plane and it was later removed by road.

Date 11 June 1948
Aircraft Avro 19 G-AGNI (ex-MG159)
Location Irish Sea
Reference 007804
Aircrew –

Shortly after taking off from Walney Island the aircraft ran out of fuel and ditched in the sea off Millom. The pilot and his passengers climbed out on to the wings of the aircraft and were rescued by a small boat. The aircraft sank a short time later. The aircraft was owned by Universal

Flying Services and was en route to the Isle of Man for the TT races.

Date 20 September 1948
Aircraft F Barracuda Mk V RK555 3 FF
Location Anthorn
Reference 164579
Aircrew Lt JI Green RN

The pilot was killed and the aircraft destroyed after it crashed on the beach at Bowness on Solway shortly after take-off from RNAS Anthorn. An investigation later proved the cause to have been the inflation of a dinghy in the cockpit, which resulted in the pilot losing control.

Date 18 October 1948
Aircraft P Proctor Mk V G-AGTD
Location Kingstown
Reference 392594
Aircrew JG Robson

After failing to become airborne during take-off, the aircraft from Astral Aviation crashed through a hedge injuring its three passengers. The aircraft was a total loss.

Date 26 November 1948
Aircraft D Dakota Mk IV KK153
Location Kirkbride
Reference 230550
Aircrew –

An oil pressure failure caused the pilot to make a forced landing on the airfield. The aircraft was on a delivery flight from 42 Sqd at RAF Bassingbourne at the time of the accident.

Date 22 June 1949
Aircraft DH Tiger Moth T5952
Location Kirkbride
Reference 230550
Aircrew –

An investigation into this forced landing was carried out by the Air Safety Board. The cause was traced to a blockage in the aircraft's fuel system. Repairs were carried out on site and the aircraft returned into service.

Date 3 August 1949
Aircraft A Anson Mk 19
Location Silloth
Reference 210785
Aircrew –

This report only identified the aircraft by its call sign which was 'Chiefy 59'; no record of its serial number was made. Its pilot made a distress call when an engine began to run rough. Air Traffic Control at Silloth gave assistance to the aircraft and talked the pilot down onto the airfield following the engine's complete failure. At the time of the incident the aircraft was en route from RAF Turnhouse to RAF Honiley.

Date 3 March 1950
Aircraft A Oxford HN176
Location Kirkbride
Reference 230550
Aircrew J Jurby

On an internal communications flight from RAF Andover, this aircraft was delivering a number of senior officers to a Commanding Officers conference when it suffered an engine failure. Its pilot made an emergency landing on the airfield, followed by a detailed inspection of the aircraft. No cause could be found for the failure and the aircraft left to complete its journey without further incident.

Date 14 April 1950
Aircraft A Lincoln RE232
Location Silloth
Reference 210785
Aircrew F/Lt RL Ducan

En route from RAF Boscombe Down to RAF Aldergrove, the aircraft crashed on take-off from Silloth following a refuelling stop. The aircraft was badly damaged and its crew of two were taken to hospital in Carlisle for treatment.

Date 26 July 1950
Aircraft H Sea Fury Mk II TF960
Location Anthorn
Reference 188588
Aircrew Lt PJ Busby RN

Flying from Lee-on-Solent an engine failure while landing caused the aircraft to undershoot the runway and crash. It turned over in soft ground killing its pilot.

Date 20 August 1950
Aircraft VS Spitfire Mk 22 PK595
607 Aux Sqd 12 Grp
Location Penrith
Reference 528188
Aircrew EA Carter
A flight of Spitfires took off from RAF Ouston and were flying west towards RAF Boulmer when the first problem occurred. The flight leader developed engine trouble and made a forced landing in a field. The remaining aircraft continued with their training flight, but on nearing Penrith this aircraft becoming low on fuel flew into poor weather conditions. Locals report hearing an aircraft fly overhead when its engine cut out. This was then followed by a whining noise and a loud explosion. The aircraft had crashed into Knipe Scar killing its pilot and making a ten-foot-deep crater. Wreckage was scattered over a wide area.

Date 24 August 1950
Aircraft V Valetta C1 VW826
Location Kirkbride
Reference 230550
Aircrew JS Luby
This aircraft was on a delivery flight to the maintenance unit at RAF Kirkbride. As the aircraft landed its port wheel broke up and the plane swung off the runway sustaining considerable damage. It was later repaired on site and returned into service.

Date 12 January 1951
Aircraft DH Vampire Mk FI VF273
203 AFS 23 Grp
Location Millom
Reference 169887
Aircrew Sgt BJ Cundall
Shortly after one in the afternoon the peace and quiet of Thwaites was disturbed by a loud explosion. It came from the area of the stone circle near Swineside. The cause was this aircraft hitting the ground at high speed, exploding scattering wreckage over a wide area. Its pilot was

killed outright. He was identified from his wallet found in the wreckage, the majority of which was removed by a salvage unit. The aircraft was on a training flight from its base at RAF Driffield when the accident occurred and was only authorised to fly within a fifty-mile radius of the airfield.

Date 8 February 1951
Aircraft DH Tiger Moth Mk II NM213
23 RMS 64 Grp
Location Stainmoor
Reference 868148
Aircrew F/O WS Bateson RAFVR
Wreckage from this aircraft can still be located on Knipe Hill. The aircraft crashed during a snowstorm on a training flight from RAF Unsworth. In the impact the pilot's safety straps broke and he was thrown clear of the aircraft into a snowdrift injuring his ankle. The crash occurred only a few miles from the pilot's home. He made his way from the wreck to a road and was given a lift to a local hospital by a passing motorist.

Date 6 June 1951
Aircraft H Tempest Mk V JN807 12 Grp
Location Low Heskit
Reference 472459
Aircrew –
The pilot of this aircraft had a remarkable escape. He was flying from RAF Acklington when his aircraft developed engine trouble. He decided to try and make an emergency landing at RAF Kirkbride, but during his approach a wing clipped a tree and the aircraft spun into the ground. The engine was torn from its mountings and the aircraft began to disintegrate, scattering wreckage over a wide area. As help arrived, the rescuers met the pilot calmly walking from the wreckage with only a small cut over his eye.

Date 22 July 1952
Aircraft M Magister G-ALGT (ex-T9889)
Location Lank Rigg
Reference 075126
Aircrew Major WL Glouster
Flying from Blackpool to Carlisle, the pilot encountered thick fog and crashed into Lank Rigg Moss, inland from St Bees. He escaped unhurt and

made his way down the fellside. Wreckage from this aircraft has been found near the crash site.

Date	17 July 1953
Aircraft	F Firefly Mk T7 WJ158
Location	Grasmere
Reference	336077
Aircrew	–

The now famous Grasmere sports field was the venue for this crash-landing. The aircraft was on an air test from RNAS Anthorn and the cause was a broken throttle linkage. The aircraft provided a new attraction for the locals until it was removed a short time later by a salvage team on a low loader.

Date	2 October 1953
Aircraft	D Skyraider AD-4B 5-53 132350
	USS *Wasp*
Location	Banner Fell
Reference	115174
Aircrew	Lt/Jg TE McDonald

This is the text of the accident report into this crash at Banner Fell:

On Friday the second of October 1953, while operating in the NATO Operation 'Mariner', the USS *Wasp* launched four aircraft of a unit from Carrier Air Group 17. They were flying a simulated low altitude attack on targets on the eastern coast of England. Two of the aircraft returned to the *Wasp* because of radio difficulties, and the remaining two aircraft carried on towards their targets. This aircraft was flying on the flight leader's starboard wing; they were to fly as low as possible an altitude from the carrier to the target 'Scampton', England and were to avoid detection by radar stations. If IFR weather conditions were encountered they were to return to the carrier.

En route they checked in over Whitehaven, the first checkpoint on the mainland mass over England. Approximately four minutes later they observed cloud covering the hill tops ahead, apparently reaching down to ground level. After consulting with his wingman on the radio the

The Fairey Firefly from RNAS Anthorn which crash-landed on Grasmere sports field. (M Daniels)

The Skyraider is unearthed on Banner Fell. The largest parts of this aircraft are covered by earth. (MJ Hurst)

An indication as to the size of the wreckage which can be found at the crash site. (MJ Hurst)

flight leader elected to abandon the mission and return to the carrier. While making a 180-degree turn to the left in company, both aircraft encountered instrument conditions. The section leader completed the turn and climbed on top of the undercast at 3,000 feet. His wingman struck the ground near the summit of a hill known as 'Banner Fell'. The section leader, after setting a course of 270 degrees 'on top' called his wingman repeatedly by radio but did not receive a reply. He alerted rescue facilities by radio and proceeded to Prestwick where he landed, and full details of the presumed accident were reported. Meanwhile the pilot of the crashed aircraft crawled clear of the wreckage when it stopped, removed his parachute and liferaft and made his way to a farmhouse approximately one mile away. He was subsequently removed to a civilian hospital where his injuries were classified as serious.

Damage to aircraft

The damage received by the aircraft as a result of the accident was strike code 'A'. The initial impact was approximately fifty feet below the summit of the hill by the propeller and fuel tanks. The mark of the first contact was forty to fifty feet long and cowling brackets were found at this point. The second point of contact was twenty-eight feet away in a straight line, and the third point of impact was approximately four hundred and thirty feet further on, where two propeller blades were found. The fourth impact point was approximately three hundred and twenty-nine feet on and larger pieces of aluminium were found together with a crushed external fuel tank, tail hook and wheel. The next point of impact was approximately one hundred and sixty feet from the final resting place of the aircraft, where two other pieces of debris were found.

At the final resting point the remaining pieces of the aircraft were found facing 180 degrees to the original path of travel. The only known witness to the accident was the pilot. Still on site are many remains from the aircraft as little was recovered; they can still be located though almost all, and certainly the large sections, was buried by the crash teams.

Date	16 October 1953
Aircraft	Dragonfly Helicopter
Location	Ulverston
Reference	298795
Aircrew	–

Extremely poor weather conditions and low visibility forced the pilot of this Royal Navy helicopter to land in Lightburn Park, Ulverston. First to locate the helicopter was the park keeper who had heard it circling overhead. The machine was undamaged and its crew unhurt. After the weather improved and numerous sightseers had been to visit, the helicopter left for its base.

Date	26 January 1954
Aircraft	B-29 (Washington) WF496
	115 Sqd
Location	Irish Sea
Reference	001734
Aircrew	–

During a training flight from its base at RAF Prestwick to the Azores, three radio messages were received from this aircraft. The first reported strong vibrations with the plane, the second advised that the plane had started to ice up, and the third advised that the crew were about to abandon the aircraft. A full-scale rescue operation was put into action with many ships and support aircraft from RAF Marham taking part. The search, centred on the last reported position which was over the Irish Sea off the coast of Cumberland, revealed nothing, but a ship in the area did find four seats from the aircraft and nothing more. In the following days some wreckage from the aircraft was washed up on beaches at the Isle of Man. Nothing more was found and the crew were never recovered. An accident investigation later concluded that the aircraft had crashed with many hours of fuel still on board, and it was thought that a fault in the fuel transfer system was the cause of the loss.

Date	24 March 1954
Aircraft	G Meteor Mk II NF WD778
	228 OTU 81 Grp
Location	Appleby
Reference	723395
Aircrew	F/O D Walker, P/O JD Briggs

Large sections of Meteor WD778 above Appleby. (MJ Hurst)

Parts of the aircraft's engine on the fell side. (MJ Hurst)

A wing from the Meteor still lies on the surface. Many other parts lie in the pools surrounding the crash site. (MJ Hurst)

The wreck of this aircraft was found by a game-keeper walking on Knock Fell. It had been taking part in a navigation training flight from its base at RAF Leeming, routing via RAF Scampton and then on to RAF Acklington. While trying to correct a course error the aircraft encountered poor weather and flew into the top of the fell. The aircraft broke up on impact killing its crew. A later examination of the wreckage indicated that they were almost out of fuel when radio contact was lost and the crash occurred. A visit to the site will still show the imprint in the soft ground where the aircraft hit; the wings and engines can also be easily found along with many other small parts. The majority of the wreckage lies buried or in small pools of water that form in the peaty ground and bogs that surround the crash site.

Date   28 October 1954
Aircraft   A Anson
Location   Kirkbride
Reference 230550
Aircrew   –

This aircraft made a crash-landing three hundred yards from the airfield near number one site. There were no injuries and the aircraft was removed to a hangar. It was later repaired by 12MU at Kirkbride and returned into service.

Date   28 October 1954
Aircraft   A Anson Mk 12 PH722 12 Grp
Location   Carlisle
Reference 375578
Aircrew   –

En route from RAF Ballenkelly to RAF Turnhouse, the aircraft experienced rough weather over the Irish Sea. Continuing, it flew into a thunderstorm near Carlisle and was hit by lightning. Many of the aircraft's instruments were knocked out by the lightning strike and the pilot decided to try and land as soon as possible. He had by now become completely lost and circled Carlisle for some time. A number of lights were put on to try and guide him to the airfield at Crosby, but he did not make the airfield and crashed near to the river at Stainton. The crew were unhurt and the wreckage was removed later by a salvage unit.

Date 13 February 1955
Aircraft Super Aero 45 TF-SOL
Location Gretna
Reference 330665
Aircrew F Olafson

The Swedish pilot of this aircraft was flying from Copenhagen to Prestwick when he lost the use of his radio compass. This was followed by an engine failure, and an emergency landing was now required. He selected a small snow-covered field near Gretna and began his descent. As he drew closer he noticed that the field was occupied by a number of sheep, which began to run around wildly as he got closer. Trying to miss the sheep he hit a low fence which caused some damage to the aircraft. The pilot was unhurt and a police guard was placed on the aircraft until it was recovered a few days later.

Date 18 August 1955
Aircraft HR-3 Dragonfly Helicopter
WG708
Location St Bees Head
Reference 958159
Aircrew –

Thick fog encompassed this helicopter en route from RNAS Anthorn to Gosport. The pilot made a forced landing on the beach at Fleswick Bay. Later that day with the weather slightly improved, the pilot flew the helicopter to the lighthouse at St Bees Head where he spent the night. He left the following day after the fog cleared, returning to his base.

Date 25 October 1955
Aircraft EE Canberra PR7 WT505
58 Sqd
Location Ponsonby Fell
Reference 081074
Aircrew F/O WE Gough, F/O D Cornforth

Police officers examining the tail section of Canberra WT505 on Ponsonby Fell.
(Ivor Nicholas, Photographer, Cockermouth).

Local people saw this aircraft flying low over the west coast of Cumberland near Sellafield, as if trying to find somewhere to land. As they watched, it made a circuit around Sellafield turned and accelerated away into low cloud and drizzle. A short time later they heard a loud explosion. The aircraft from RAF Wyton had crashed on Ponsonby Fell near Gaite Kirk, killing its crew. The majority of the wreckage was removed after the accident but some parts have been found in the area.

Date 20 January 1956
Aircraft B-29 Superfortress 461600
53 WRS USAF
Location Kendal
Reference 570835
Aircrew Major B Hilkman
Flying a weather reconnaissance mission from its base at USAF Burtonwood, this aircraft flew into the North Atlantic airspace. The flight was uneventful until the return journey was started

and two of the aircraft's engines began to run roughly. The pilot advised the authorities of the situation and was diverted to RAF Prestwick. However, as they neared Prestwick the engines recovered and the pilot decided to try and return to his home base. Nearing Kendal the engines again started to give problems and the crew decided to abandon the aircraft. After locking in a course that would have taken the aircraft out to sea, the crew began to leave the plane. As they descended in their parachutes they saw the aircraft begin to turn from its course and circle, almost running into them before it crashed near Tarnhouse reservoir. The crew landed in the same area with only minor injuries, and a guard was placed on the wreckage until it was removed by road. Nothing can be seen at the crash site now as it is very accessible; however, the author did find one of the crew's parachute packs in a gorse bush in 1971. With the still readable markings on the chute pack it was traced back to the USAF at Burtonwood.

The author examines a parachute pack found at the crash site of the Superfortress near Kendal
(MJ Hurst)

Date 6 February 1956
Aircraft EE Canberra WM715
Location Haverigg
Reference 140790
Aircrew W/Cdr D De-Villers

Airborne from BAC Warton this aircraft was on an air test being piloted by the then English Electric chief test pilot. The aircraft suffered technical difficulties and the pilot made a successful landing on the now disused airfield at Haverigg. Some damage was sustained by the undercarriage, which was repaired on site and the aircraft was flown out a short time later.

Date 12 July 1956
Aircraft F Firefly Mk T7 WM803
Location Bowness on Solway
Reference 223630
Aircrew –

Another aircraft which was on an air test, this time from RNAS Anthorn. The aircraft suffered an engine failure and the pilot made a forced landing on the sands at Bowness on Solway. The pilot was unhurt and the aircraft undamaged. Local people used a tractor to pull the aircraft up the beach and on to the road before the tide came in.

Date 23 October 1956
Aircraft DH Vampire Mk Fb4 WR553
Location Silloth
Reference 136550
Aircrew F/O R Marks

Thick black smoke was pouring from this aircraft's engine during a flight from RAF Silloth. The pilot began an approach to land at the airfield but was unable to maintain height. He failed to reach the airfield and crash-landed on the marshy ground at Skinburness. The aircraft crossed a road and ran into a small dyke at the perimeter of the airfield.

Date 4 March 1957
Aircraft DH Venom Mk Fb4 WR557
22 MU 41 Grp
Location Croglin Fell
Reference 642470
Aircrew F/Lt WF Marshall

The duty air traffic controller at RAF Silloth received an SOS from the pilot of this aircraft.

The Vampire nestling in the dyke short of Silloth airfield. (Crown copyright)

– 89 –

He reported that his elevators had jammed and there were no further communications with the aircraft. Air traffic control knew that the pilot was engaged on a training flight east of Carlisle, and a full-scale search and rescue operation was started. The search continued for three days until the wreckage was spotted by a helicopter pilot from RNAS Anthorn. The aircraft had crashed near Lawer's Cross, Croglin Fell killing its pilot. A guard was placed on the wreckage until an investigation had been carried out. Most of the larger parts were removed or buried at the site, although some parts can still be easily located today.

Date	24 May 1959
Aircraft	DH Tiger Moth G-APFS
Location	Broughton in Furness
Reference	227868
Aircrew	RS Milson

Three aircraft were carrying out crop spraying operations near Wreaks Moss, each aircraft carrying a four hundredweight load of lime. The routine was for the aircraft to take-off, carry out the 'dressing' and then return to re-load. During the take-off run one of the pilots realised that he would not be able to get airborne and tried to jettison his load. Unfortunately he was too late and the aircraft nose dived into the field. The pilot was shaken but unhurt; the aircraft, however, was badly damaged. Its undercarriage was completely torn off, a wing was twisted and the propeller smashed. The wreckage was removed by road for repair in Portsmouth and the other aircraft continued crop spraying.

Date	29 June 1959
Aircraft	NA Sabre Mk 6 23380 421 Sqd RCAF
Location	Iron Cragg
Reference	121117
Aircrew	F/O RG Starling RCAF

Many parts from this aircraft can still be seen on Iron Cragg, where it crashed killing its pilot during a flight from RAF Prestwick to RAF Northolt. The aircraft and pilot were en route to join their squadron in France when the crash

occurred. The aircraft's tail can still be seen among boulders and the engine is close to a sheep pen. One of the aircraft's cannons was found beside a stone wall in 1962.

Date	19 November 1959
Aircraft	DH Tiger Moth G-APFS
Location	Ulverston
Reference	299795
Aircrew	–

Having just completed a repair following a previous accident in May this Tiger Moth was returning to carry out crop spraying work in the Lakes. Before it could do so the aircraft hit an electricity pylon near Ness Farm, Newlands at Ulverston which caused it to spin into a small ditch. Local people were quickly on the scene to help the pilot who was treated for shock by a local doctor. Once again the aircraft was removed by road, presumably for yet another repair.

Date	9 March 1960
Aircraft	G Javelin Mk 8 XH988 41 Sqd
Location	Durdar
Reference	402514
Aircrew	–

The two-man crew of this aircraft ejected when they were unable to re-start its engines following a double flame-out during a flight from RAF Wattisham to a base in Scotland. The plane crashed into a field near Crownstone Farm and exploded, badly frightening a farm worker who was ploughing a field as the aircraft came down. Wreckage was thrown over a wide area, the largest piece being only a few feet in size. The crew landed safely about a mile away with only minor injuries associated with an ejection. A strong police guard was placed on the wreckage until it was removed by road.

Date	28 October 1960
Aircraft	Unidentified
Location	Appleby
Reference	Unknown
Aircrew	–

An unidentified aircraft made a forced landing in a field close to the village. Apart from the police report little other information is available.

Date 4 November 1960
Aircraft A Auster G-AMMZ
Location Brough
Reference 787145
Aircrew WS Bateson

This pilot was not a lucky man. Some years earlier (8/2/51) he was involved in an almost identical accident to this only a short distance away from this location. As he was taking off, the aircraft's engine failed causing it to strike a fence at the end of a small field and overturn. Fortunately there was no fire and all escaped with only minor injuries. A few years later the pilot was killed in a flying accident at Blackpool.

Date 3 February 1961
Aircraft F-101 Voodoo 41456 81 TFW USAF
Location Solway Firth
Reference 040520
Aircrew 1st Lt RS Nishibayshi

In the sea between Maryport and Silloth lie the remains of this aircraft. The aircraft crashed during a training flight, killing its pilot. The aircraft was from USAF Woodbridge and its pilot was from Honolulu. For some weeks after the accident fragments of the aircraft were washed up on the beach near Maryport.

Date 22 February 1961
Aircraft A Auster G-AJEH
Location Workington
Reference 009256
Aircrew –

A forced landing at Low Scales farm was made by this pilot following a fuel shortage. There were no injuries or damage and the aircraft was flown out following a refuelling exercise.

Date 28 July 1961
Aircraft A Auster G-AMTE
Location Crosby
Reference 480605
Aircrew –

Pilot error was the reported cause of this aircraft crashing onto the runway at Crosby in the early evening. Its crew were unhurt though the aircraft was damaged.

Date 17 October 1961
Aircraft DC-3 Dakota G-AMVC
Location Croglin Fell
Reference 595496
Aircrew Cpt HE Mose, CN Wildman, A Francis, V Christian

A civilian aircraft belonging to BKS Air Transport crashed in poor weather conditions near the Silver Band, Croglin Fell killing all of its crew. The aircraft was en route from Yeadon to Carlisle to collect passengers and was heard to fly overhead Crosby airfield at nine o'clock. The last radio contact was made at 9.35 and no further contact was made. Later, villagers from Croglin reported that an aircraft passed overhead, followed by an explosion high on the fell. A search and rescue operation was put into action immediately. The wreckage was located by a helicopter from RAF Acklington and rescue teams found a trail of wreckage stretching over a hundred yards. The wings had been torn off and the bottom of the aircraft ripped out. Three of its crew were found near the aircraft and the fourth was found some considerable distance away. A visit to the site will still show some remains from the wreckage although it is now difficult to find. Some of the wreckage was buried on site while other parts were removed.

Date 12 April 1962
Aircraft A Anson Mk 19 TX219
Location Carlisle
Reference 480605
Aircrew –

The crew of this aircraft escaped unhurt after its undercarriage collapsed during a landing at the airfield. Repairs were carried out on site and the plane returned to its station.

Date 25 September 1962
Aircraft A Auster G-AMTE
Location Longtown
Reference 353653
Aircrew –

Following a previous accident at Crosby in July the aircraft suffered an engine failure shortly after take-off. The pilot made a forced landing near Mossbank House. The crew were unhurt and repairs were carried out later.

Bodies of the crew are removed from the wreckage of the crashed Dakota on Croglin Fell. (Robert Armstrong)

The bottom was torn out of the Dakota as it crashed into the fell side. (Robert Armstrong)

Date	29 January 1963
Aircraft	EE Canberra PR7 WJ824 57 Sqd
Location	High Pike
Reference	367352
Aircrew	F/Lt L Broughton,
	Sqd Ldr JC Almond

Wreckage from this aircraft was scattered over a mile and a half after it exploded on High Pike, Caldbeck killing its crew. Local farmers acted as guides for the police and rescue teams from RAF Leeming. The crew members were found still strapped in their ejection seats a hundred yards from the summit. The largest section remaining was the aircraft's tailplane. Some sections and parts of the aircraft can still be found in the area though much was removed.

Date	8 July 1965
Aircraft	EE Lightning Mk T4 / T5 XM966
Location	Whitehaven
Reference	931308
Aircrew	J Dell, G Elkinton

A structural failure during a scheduled test flight at thirty thousand feet left the pilot with little control over the plane and little other option than to eject from his aircraft with his crewman. The ejection was faultless and they landed close together in the Irish Sea. The flight was being monitored by radar and a search and rescue operation was underway almost before the crew hit the water. The crew were located by a Canberra aircraft from Warton and then monitored by Shackleton from RAF Kinloss. The crew were picked up by helicopter and taken to hospital. In the following days an extensive search of the sea bed was carried out by trawlers and naval vessels. The material they recovered was to prove valuable in the subsequent investigation. This aircraft was the prototype conversion for the T5 aircraft XM967.

Date	22 February 1966
Aircraft	Cessna 150 G-ASYH
Location	Black Combe
Reference	850137
Aircrew	–

The ventral tank from the crashed Lightning being brought ashore at Whitehaven.
(Ivor Nicholas, Photographer, Cockermouth)

The wreckage of Cessna G-ASYH on Black Coombe. (Ivor Nicholas, Photographer, Cockermouth)

Airborne from Blackpool this aircraft flew into poor weather and crashed four hundred yards south-west of the trig point on Black Combe. Its crew of two were killed outright. It took search teams some days to locate the crash site, and the majority of the remains have now been removed though some fragments have been seen at the site.

Date   3 September 1966
Aircraft   Cessna 150 G-ATSS
Location   Bootle
Reference   135845
Aircrew   –

An engine failure caused this forced landing in a field near Syke Beck Farm, Bootle. The pilot was unhurt and the aircraft undamaged.

Date   17 September 1966
Aircraft   P Cherokee G-ASKE
Location   Esk House
Reference   228081
Aircrew   G Massie, L Aitchison

Overdue on a flight from Millfield the aircraft was posted missing by air traffic control. A search later found the plane on Esk House after it crashed in poor weather killing its crew. The pilot had managed to clear one ridge but then struck a large rock outcrop while descending into a valley. The wreck was first reached by an RAF Mountain Rescue team which was on exercise in the area. A climb to the site will still show remains of the aircraft.

Date   4 February 1967
Aircraft   P Colt G-ARNH
Location   Silloth
Reference   126542
Aircrew   –

Strong winds with gale force gusts caused the pilot to make a forced landing on the now disused airfield at Silloth. The aircraft was able to leave the following day after the weather improved.

Date 23 September 1967
Aircraft Cessna 150 G-ARFN
Location Newby East
Reference 472583
Aircrew −

Following an engine failure on take-off this aircraft crashed in a field north of the airfield at Newby. It overturned and came to rest against a small bank. The crew escaped without injury.

Date 6 July 1969
Aircraft Dart Herald G-APWB
Location Carlisle
Reference 480605
Aircrew −

An engine malfunction caused this forced landing at Crosby. There was no damage to the aircraft and, following repairs to its engine, it left a few days later.

Date 8 July 1969
Aircraft Cessna 150
Location Carlisle
Reference 480605
Aircrew −

Another engine failure after take-off followed by another forced landing, this time in a field adjacent to the Newby East road. The identity of the aircraft was not recorded.

Date 10 July 1969
Aircraft Dart Herald
Location Carlisle
Reference 480605
Aircrew −

After a warning light came on in the cockpit, the pilot elected to make an emergency landing at Crosby. Investigation proved no fault and the aircraft continued its journey later.

Date 11 July 1970
Aircraft SA Rallye G-AXIT
Location Workington
Reference 989261
Aircrew −

Poor weather caused the pilot to make a forced landing at Salterbeck next to the cemetery. Once the weather improved the pilot continued his journey.

Date 10 December 1970
Aircraft PA 28 Cherokee G-AYKV
Location Carlisle
Reference 480605
Aircrew −

Poor weather and an inexperienced pilot contributed to this emergency landing at Crosby. There was no damage or injury recorded.

A badly parked Cessna at Newby East. (J Huggon)

A Rallye at Workington prepares to leave following an improvement in the weather.
(Ivor Nicholas, Photographer, Cockermouth)

Date   1 December 1971
Aircraft   Sioux Helicopter XT202 3 MC
    Sioux Helicopter XT213 3 MC
    Sioux Helicopter XT844 3 MC
Location   Heversham
Reference   495832
Aircrew   Cpt D Storrie (OC)

Flying to their base in Northern Ireland, these helicopters encountered poor weather conditions and low visibility near Milnthorpe. They made a forced landing in a field near the Blue Bell Inn at Heversham. The helicopters provided interest for pupils at the local grammar school before they left to continue their journey once the weather improved.

Date   5 July 1972
Aircraft   Sioux Helicopter XT105
Location   Kendal
Reference   531968
Aircrew   –

En route from Blackpool to RAF Aldergrove in Northern Ireland the pilot was forced to make a landing north of Kendal due to poor weather and low visibility. After obtaining his location he lifted off and flew south over Kendal at a low altitude keeping below the low cloud cover. This

incident was witnessed by the author who was driving between Kendal and Penrith at the time.

Date   21 November 1972
Aircraft   McD Phantom Mk FGR2 XV477
    6 Sqd
Location   Thack Moor
Reference   651462
Aircrew   F/Lt CM Haynes, F/Lt M Smith

Two Phantom aircraft were flying from RAF Conningsby on a low-level training flight over the Lake District when they encountered poor weather and low cloud near Penrith. As the aircraft pulled up through the cloud only one emerged on top; unable to make contact with his wing man the second aircraft put out a distress call. An air-sea rescue operation was put into action involving teams from RAF Leeming, Stafford and Leuchars. The wreckage of the Phantom was located shortly after ten in the evening. It had hit the ground only sixty feet short of the summit of Thack Moor, near Croglin Fell, and exploded killing the crew. The wreckage was removed by salvage units following an intensive recovery programme and taken to RAE Farnborough were it was rebuilt for the crash investigation that followed.

Three Sioux helicopters at Heversham provide a talking point for pupils at the local grammar school. (Westmorland Gazette)

The wing of Phantom XV477 on Thack Moor. (J Huggon)

Date 8 December 1972
Aircraft Cessna 172k G-AYDC
Location Flookbrough
Reference 389730
Aircrew A Lindly

The young pilot of this French-built Cessna was killed during a flight from Blackpool to Cark when the plane crashed into the sea off Humphrey Head. Rescuers were unable to reach the aircraft until the tide had gone out. An investigation later proved the crash to have been caused by the aircraft's carburettor icing up while flying through a snowstorm, and the inexperience of its pilot.

Date 25 March 1973
Aircraft PA-28 Cherokee G-AZYP
Location Wastwater
Reference 164049
Aircrew –

Returning from Kirkbride to Blackpool, the four crew members of this Cherokee were killed when the aircraft crashed into the face of Ill Gill Head. Rescue teams had difficulty in reaching the crash site because of the terrain. A climb to the site today will show many remains from the aircraft among the rocks on the scree slope and in the small tarn below.

An investigation into the crash found the aircraft was climbing very steeply under full throttle at the time of impact. The aircraft belonged to the Air Navigation and Trading Aero Club from Blackpool.

Date 31 July 1973
Aircraft Beagle Pup G-AXIC
Location Keswick
Reference 263229
Aircrew –

This accident caused quite a stir at the time. The pilot took the aircraft from an airfield near London and went on a 'jolly'. He was seen to fly under Tower Bridge, and in and out of large tower blocks in the city before he headed north. Police were put on a nationwide alert to find the aircraft. His daredevil flight was to end in a car

The Phantom's point of impact. (J Huggon)

The wreckage of Beagle Pup short of the car park at Keswick. (Lakeland Photographers)

park at Keswick. As he approached the car park the wing of the aircraft struck a large tree causing the plane to spin into the ground. Had it not, the aircraft might well have hit people and cars in the crowded car park. The pilot was killed and the aircraft completely destroyed.

Date 5 May 1975
Aircraft F-111 UH F081 99 TAW USAF
Location Shap Fell
Reference 529070
Aircrew –

The majority of the crash reports in this book have been visited months and years after the

event. In this case I was able to visit the crash site within a few hours of it happening. Together with cadets from Windermere ATC we were shown around the crash site by members of the American Air Force who formed the recovery and crash investigation team from USAF Upper Heyford. Problems started for the crew of this aircraft after it struck a bird during a low-level flight. After passing through the armoured windscreen the bird hit the crew and started a chain of events that led to the crash. The remains of the hapless bird exited the cockpit and went down an engine intake; at this point the crew ejected from the nose section of the fuselage and landed

The wing of the F-111 on Shap Fell. (MJ Hurst)

The author and a member of the crash team inspect a piece of the wreckage sticking out from the soft ground. (MJ Hurst)

unhurt near the summit of Shap Fell. The aircraft then crashed and exploded four miles from the road scattering wreckage over a wide area. The impact caused a crater some eight feet in depth, with large sections of the aircraft sticking out of the soft ground like fingers. The wreckage was removed by helicopter to the main road and taken away on low loaders. A visit now will show very little and the exact position can be difficult to locate.

Date	18 January 1976
Aircraft	Cessna 172H G-AWMZ
Location	Burn Moor
Reference	145924
Aircrew	–

The crater at the impact site.
(MJ Hurst)

Odd remains from the Phantom crash site at Mawbray. (MJ Hurst)

Four passengers had a lucky escape when this aircraft hit the top of Burn Moor and crashed. The aircraft was on a business flight returning to Blackpool when it encountered low cloud after crossing the coast. While the pilot was trying to locate his position, he flew into the fellside only a few feet from the summit and overturned. He then made his way down to the road to a telephone box where he summoned help. Rescue teams brought the remaining passengers to safety.

Date 31 March 1976
Aircraft Piper PA-28 G-ABBPY
Location Silloth
Reference 126542
Aircrew –

The wing of this aircraft struck a parked car after landing at the disused airfield at Kirkbride. There were no injuries to the crew and damage to the aircraft was slight.

Date 10 May 1976
Aircraft Piper PA-39
Location Carlisle
Reference –
Aircrew –

During a night landing the pilot of this aircraft mistakenly raised the undercarriage instead of the aircraft's flaps. The pilot crashed onto the runway at Crosby. Fortunately the crew suffered no injuries and the aircraft was later recovered.

Date –
Aircraft McD Phantom
Location Mawbray
Reference 082474

This account was given by a resident of the village: 'I saw the aircraft coming in low over the village and banking steeply. It was making a strange noise. As it flew over the beach a wing hit the ground and it crashed. There was a bright flash which lit up the village even in broad daylight, which was followed by a terrific explosion.' Wreckage was thrown over a wide area of the beach and the crew of two died instantly. An exacting recovery operation followed and the area was kept under observation for some months so that wreckage or armaments could be recovered.

RAF Haverigg. An aerial photograph taken from 22,000 ft during 1944. Up to forty aircraft can be seen on the airfield. (Public Record Office at Kew)

(Left) *This propeller came from an Avro Anson which was found on Lords Seat near Keswick.* (MJ Hurst)

(Below) *Searching old airfield dispersals and bunkers also provided some interesting finds, such as this Meteor damaged in an airfield accident.* (MJ Hurst)

(Above) *After trekking miles across the fells, the first signs of a crash site are located.* (MJ Hurst)

(Left) *The author traced crash sites not only from the ground but also from the air.* (MJ Hurst)

Before starting the survey of aircraft wrecks in the Lakes, members of the team underwent intensive training in expedition, survival and search techniques. (MJ Hurst)

Unidentified remains found on Wild Boar Fell. (MJ Hurst)

Chapter Four

Unidentified and missing aircraft

Date 1 April 1940
Aircraft Unknown
Location –
Reference –
Aircraft missing in Cumbria, not located.

Date 1940 / 1941
Aircraft B Blenheim
Location Whitehaven
Reference Unknown
A local resident recalled this aircraft crashing on the beach at Braystones during the night. The aircraft was on a flight from the Isle of Man. The resident had the pilot's safety harness from the aircraft as tangible evidence of the accident. However, the date and aircraft number are not known.

Date 10 December 1941
Aircraft VS Spitfire MkV AR475
Location –
Reference –
ATA pilot flying from Speke to Prestwick lost over the Lake District. Not located.

Date 19 December 1941
Aircraft Unknown
Location –
Reference –
Medium bomber crashed near the boundary stone on Lecke Fell, Tebay. Crew killed.

Date 1942
Aircraft V Walrus
Location Distington
Reference Unknown
A Vickers Walrus seaplane made a crash-landing in a field next to the Distington to Gilgarran road. The incident was recalled by local people.

Date 1942
Aircraft H Hind or Hart
Location Whitehaven
Reference –
The same people also recall a Hawker Hind type of aircraft crashing and overturning in a field near Mirehouse Pond. They recalled that it had a heavy guard placed on it until its removal.

Date 13 January 1942
Aircraft M Magister Mk I P2468
Location Millom
Reference Unknown
Police report of an aircraft crashing near Millom. No other information is recorded.

Date 18 March 1942
Aircraft HP Hampden P3130
Location Unknown
Reference –
Flying from Kirkbride to RAF Harwarden, lost over Lake District, not located.

Date 3 November 1943
Aircraft Unknown
Location Unknown
Reference –
Two aircrew were killed when this aircraft from RAF Crosby crashed.

Date 1943
Aircraft F Barracuda
Location Seascale
Reference –
This aircraft force-landed on the beach at Seascale. No other details are recorded.

Date 1943
Aircraft AW Whitley Mk 11 Z9362 24 OTU
Location Solway off Saltcotes Pier
Reference 260970
Aircrew F/O JCN Lewis 109536

Other than the aircraft crash-landing and sinking two miles off Saltcotes Pier, and the body of this airman being recovered, little else of the incident is recorded.

Date 1944
Aircraft M Master Mk III
Location Cark
Reference 395748
This account was also provided by the Officer Commanding the Mountain Rescue unit at RAF Cark:

A Polish pilot from RAF Walney Island had an engine failure near Cark. The pilot saw the vast expanse of sand and decided to force-land. The minute he touched down the aircraft went up on its nose killing the pilot due to the sudden stop. The tide was coming in and as the sands in that area are quicksands, the aircraft sank. The crash had been seen by local people but no one reported it to Cark for over five hours. We received the information on the crash and a team led by myself went to the area. We found the aircraft with its cockpit closed and sand all over the machine and up to the top of the cockpit. We tried to attach ropes to any part of the aircraft but could not; I myself did everything I knew to open the cockpit cover, but as I worked the aircraft sank lower into the sand and in the end I was pulled clear of the aircraft. The Navy was called in and their answer was 'nothing can be done, leave it'. For weeks I visited the site at low tide but I could do absolutely nothing.

Date 19 January 1945
Aircraft DH Tiger Moth Mk II T5960
DH Tiger Moth Mk I N9160
Location Unknown
Reference Unknown
The location of these crash sites is unrecorded. There is a record in the station log, and police reports of them being destroyed in a mid-air collision in the Lake District on the 19th.

Date 12 March 1945
Aircraft Unknown
Location Bootle
Reference –
Aircraft reported to be down at or near Bootle.

Date 31 May 1945
Aircraft Unknown
Location Allonby
Reference –
Aircraft reported as crashed near Allonby.

Date 30 May 1945
Aircraft Unknown
Location Unknown
Reference Unknown
Another report taken from police records, and an entry in the station diary, but no firm information was recorded. The aircraft was noted as having crashed in the Lake District.

Date 1945
Aircraft DH Tiger Moth Mk II T6930
Location Unknown
Reference Unknown
A report of this aircraft crashing was entered in police records, but no other information was available.

Date 10 June 1946
Aircraft Unknown
Location Off Whitehaven
Reference Unknown
Seen to crash into the sea by a local inshore fisherman. No trace of this aircraft was found.

Date 1951
Aircraft Aeronca 100
Location Irish Sea
Reference –
A newspaper reports this aircraft as being lost in the Irish Sea off Silecroft. Despite a search nothing was found.

Date 1956
Aircraft M Magister N3775 / G-AKPE
Location Carlisle
Reference –
There is a record advising that this aircraft was destroyed in a gale, at Carlisle in 1956. It is assumed that it was at Kingstown and was an ex-RAF aircraft sold to a civilian company who left it unattended at the station for a number of months. No firm details are available.

Date 28 October 1960
Aircraft Unidentified
Location Appleby
Reference Unknown

An unidentified aircraft made a forced landing in a field close to the village. Apart from the police report little other information is available.

Date Uncertain
Aircraft VS Spitfire
Location Unknown
Reference May have been Coniston

The following report was received from the then Commanding Officer of RAF Cark's Mountain Rescue Team:

The incident of the lost Spitfire was a curious thing. RAF Cark started a mountain rescue training section. We trained teams that went out to the Far East and also around Britain. On one of our training climbs we found a Spitfire. The aircraft was upside down on the ground, its pilot had killed himself by flying onto the ground. His neck was broken and we traced the date of take-off from a Scottish station. The pilot was delivering the machine to his squadron. We brought the aeroplane down to Cark by taking off the wings, removing the engine first of all; it was a tricky job. There was very little damage, and the aircraft was rebuilt at RAF Cark. We found the machine exactly one year to the day after it was reported as missing. The body of the pilot was brought down and returned to his home town for burial.

Date Unknown
Location Unknown
Reference Unknown

Little information is recorded on this accident, other than an entry in the Register of Deaths. The aircraft crashed killing its pilot.

Date Uncertain
Aircraft W Lysander
Location Cockermouth
Reference Unknown

Again a local resident recalls visiting the aircraft which made a forced landing near Cockermouth Castle. Unfortunately he does not remember the date of the incident.

Date Unknown
Aircraft F Battle
Location Millom
Reference –

The following account was provided a couple of years ago by the navigator of a Fairey Battle which crash-landed in the sea off Millom.

The aircraft was returning to RAF Haverigg after completing a practice bombing exercise on the range at Sealand near the Mull of Galloway. The conversation went as follows:
Pilot: We're running low on fuel,
Nav: 'Have we enough to make Millom?'
Pilot: 'No, I will try and make height.'
Nav: 'OK, I'll plot our position.'
Pilot: 'You get ready to jump.'
Nav: 'Are you going to jump, then?'
Pilot: 'No.'
Nav: 'Then neither am I. I'll get my bloody feet wet if I do.'
The engine cut and the pilot put the aircraft down on the water to make a copybook pancake. The only injury was that, on touchdown, the navigator bumped his head. The date as far as I can recall was January or February 1940. The two crew were picked up by an air-sea rescue boat and the aircraft was recovered and later returned into service.

The fuel shortage was traced to a loose union somewhere in the fuel system. The pilot was later killed in another Battle on approach to Millom.

Date Uncertain
Aircraft Unknown
Location Wild Boar Fell
Reference –

Police report an aircraft seen to nose dive into Wild Boar Fell approximately six miles south of Kirby Stephen; not located.

Air Crashes in the Lake District

The following collection of locations has been provided by farmers, fell walkers and shepherds who have found wreckage during the course of their walks. Some are confirmed by police reports but none has been positively identified:

Bandreath Crag	118248	Wreckage found	
Bow Scale Fell	Wreckage found in bog by shepherd		
Birkdale Fell	780266	Appleby, 28-10-40	
Northmoor	7-10-42	H Hurricane	
Dent area	259737	842813	776804	790895
Great Coombe	828702		

Chapter Five

Airfield Construction Plans

Airfield Construction Plans

During the research of information for this book, a number of airfield construction plans were discovered. A number of these for airfields situated in the area covered by the book have been included. The reader may wish to compare the aerial photograph of RAF Haverigg with the airfield plan for Millom. The majority of these airfields are now disused and the surrounding countryside, fields and buildings have changed quite considerably. The airfields, satellite landing grounds and flying boat factory which were operational within the area covered by the book were:

RAF Silloth	RAF Kirkbride
RAF Longtown	RAF Crosby
RAF Kingstown	RAF Cark
RAF Walney Island	RNAS Anthorn
White Cross Bay	39 SLG Brayton
SLG Burnfoot	SLG Hornby
10 SLG Wath Head	

RAF Kingstown (Carlisle)

Listed as Carlisle this airfield was a grass field and home to 15 EFTS (Elementary Flying Training School). The two main hangars can be seen to the east of the airfield on the main technical site. Seven ammunition and fuel dumps can be seen to the east and south-west corners of the airfield, with a further four to the north. The inset at the bottom of the field is Lowery Hill Farm which was the crash site of an Avro Anson in

November 1940; to the east of the airfield running north to south is the main north coast LNER railway line.

Stannis cemetery can be seen to the lower south-east of the plan. No building work was carried out at site No. 2, which was de-requisitioned in July 1944. The main feature is the A7 trunk road from Carlisle to Edinburgh also running north to south. The fork left by the technical site becomes the A74 to Annan.

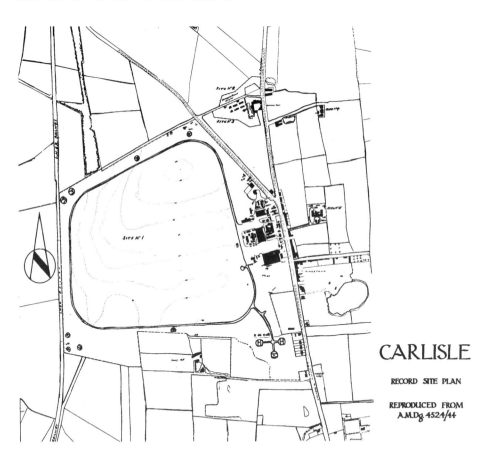

CARLISLE

RECORD SITE PLAN

REPRODUCED FROM
A.M.Dg 4524/44

RAF Crosby (Carlisle civil airport)

Now Carlisle airport, Crosby was a very active airfield during the war. Its seven main hangars can be clearly seen along with the dispersal areas, fuel and ammunition bunkers. At the extreme south of the airfield is the B6264 Carlisle to Brampton road, to the east of the airfield is 'Beanlands Park' which saw a number of crash-landings. The course of a Roman road runs through the airfield and to the north can be seen the course of Hadrian's Wall and its Vallum. The main technical site can be easily seen to the north of the runways; the other sites for this airfield are mainly to the north of the Wall and Vallum.

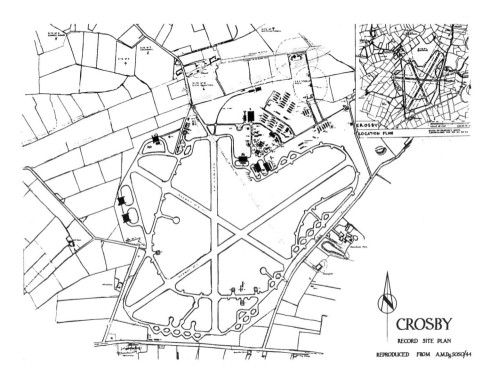

CROSBY

RECORD SITE PLAN

REPRODUCED FROM A.M.D₅ 5050/44

RAF Kirkbride

Kirkbride and Silloth represented the largest of the airfields in the Lake District. As the reader will see Kirkbride was a well dispersed airfield. Some of the hard standings and hangars were situated some two miles south of the main site.

Fifteen hangars can be easily identified along with the dispersal sites. The main technical area was to the north-west of runway 10/28. Powhill is shown just below the two hangars at site 'D' which was north-west of the airfield. The insert plans show blister hangars, Robins and Super Robins and Bellmouth hard standings well over two miles from the main airfield site.

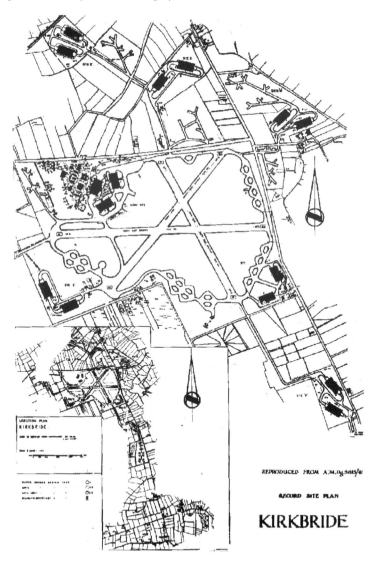

KIRKBRIDE

RAF Walney Island (Barrow)

Although not strictly in the author's Lake District, Walney Island has been included as a number of aircraft operating from the station were lost in the Lakes. The airfield is situated at the northernmost point of Walney Island to the west of Barrow in Furness. Walney is a larger airfield than most expect, with ten sites which

extended south of North Scale. The three main hangars can be seen in the main technical area to the south-east of Runway No. 1. To the north of runway No. 2 are the fuel and munitions bunkers; the dispersal areas can also be easily found. Situated to the north-west of runway No. 2 were the rifle butts and ranges.

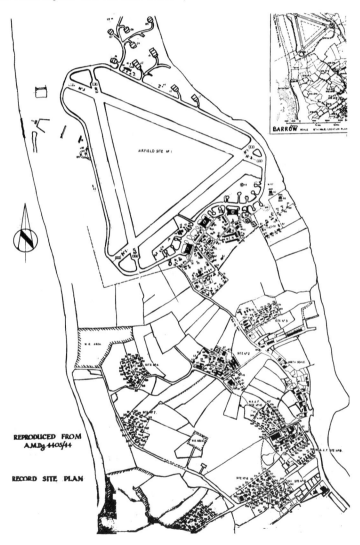

RAF Haverigg (Millom)

Situated to the west of Millom this station is now a high security prison. Its eight hangars to the north-west of the technical site can be easily seen on the plan. The reader may like to compare the plan with an aerial photograph of installation in the previous chapter. Fuel and ammunition bunkers can be seen around the perimeter track of the airfield interspersed with dispersal strips. To the south-east of runway 35 were the rifle range and moving target ranges for the station. A short distance inland from Haverigg is Black Combe which claimed a number of aircraft during and after the war. Between the two is High Low Scales onto which an American B-17 crashed. From time to time, and mainly following storms, the remains of aircraft are still found on the beaches around this area washed ashore from many aircraft lost in the sea.

RECORD SITE PLAN

MILLOM

RAF Cark

Another station in the south of the Lakes was RAF Cark, home to a Special Pilot Training Unit. For some time it operated a varied number of aircraft types, and a mountain rescue section.

The airfield is just south of Flookbrough; its main technical site was just north of runway No. 1, and slightly further north of this can be seen the fuel and ammunition bunkers.

Additional bunkers were also sited around the perimiter track to the west of the airfield.

At the extreme south of the plan is East Plain Farm; to its north-east was the site of an army detachment camp. To the north of the plan was site No. 7, the station's sick quarters. South of the sick quarters were the WRAF quarters site No. 6 and the station's communal area site No. 2.

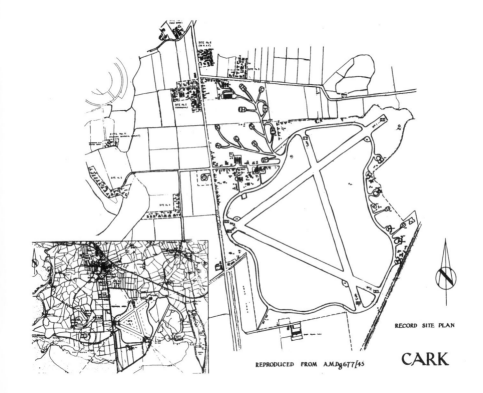

RECORD SITE PLAN

REPRODUCED FROM A.M.Dg 677/45

CARK

Glossary

1st Lt	First Lieutenant USAF	M	Miles
A	Avro / Airspeed	MC	Marine Corps
AEF	Air Experience Flight	McD	McDonnell Douglas
AFS	Affiliated Fighter Squadron	MU	Maintenance Unit
AFU	Auxiliary Flying Unit	NA	North American
AGS	Air Gunnery School	NZ	New Zealand
ANO	Another (Unidentified)	OCU	Operational Conversion Unit
AOS	Air Observation School	OTU	Operational Training Unit
ATA	Air Transport Auxiliary	P/O	Pilot Officer
ATC	Air Training Corps	PAF	Polish Air Force
ATW	Air Tactical Wing	PA	Piper Aircraft
AUS	Prefix to aircrew serial number used by RAAF	PR	Photographic Reconnaissance
		PRC	Pilot Refresher Course
AW	Armstrong Whitworth	r	Prefix to aircrew serial number used by RCAF
B	Blackburn / Bristol		
BP	Boulton Paul	RAF	Royal Air Force
COTU	Coastal Operations Training Unit	RCAF	Royal Canadian Air Force
Cpt	Captain	RNAS	Royal Naval Air Station
DH	De Havilland	RNVR	Royal Naval Volunteer Reserve
EE	English Electric	RNZAF	Royal New Zealand Air Force
EFTS	Elementary Flying Training School	S	Shorts
Eng	Engineer	Sgt	Sergeant
F	Fairey	SLG	Satellite Landing Ground
F/Lt	Flight Lieutenant	SPTU	Special Pilot Training Unit
F/O	Flying Officer	Sqd	Squadron
F/Sgt	Flight Sergeant	Sqd/Ldr	Squadron Leader
ff	Prefix to aircrew serial number used by FFAF	TB	Torpedo Bomber
		TEU	Tactical Exercise Unit
G	Gloucester	TFU	Tactical Fighter Unit
Grp	Group	USAAF	United States Army Air Force
H	Hawker	USAF	United States Air Force
HCU	Heavy Conversion Unit	USS	United States Ship
HP	Handley Page	VS	Vickers Supermarine
IMC	Instrument meteorological conditions	W	Westland
j	Prefix to aircrew serial number used by RCAF	W/Cdr	Wing Commander
		W/O	Warrant Officer
L	Lockheed	W/O2	Warrant Officer second class
LAC	Leading Aircraftsman	WRS	Weather Reconnaissance Squadron